BRANDO'S
BRIDE

**The Incredibly True Story of Anna Kashfi
and Her Marriage to One of Hollywood's
Greatest Stars**

Sarah Broughton is an award-winning writer, researcher and producer. She lives in Cardiff.

She has also written a novel, Other Useful Numbers.

BRANDO'S BRIDE

The Incredibly True Story of Anna Kashfi and Her Marriage to One of Hollywood's Greatest Stars

SARAH BROUGHTON

PARTHIAN

Parthian, Cardigan SA43 1ED
www.parthianbooks.com
First published in 2019
© Sarah Broughton 2019
ISBN 978-1-912681-27-3
Editor: Richard Davies
Cover design by www.theundercard.co.uk
Typeset by Elaine Sharples
Printed and bound by 4edge Limited, UK
Published with the financial support of the Welsh Books Council
British Library Cataloguing in Publication Data
A cataloguing record for this book is available from
the British Library.
Every attempt has been made to secure the permission of
copyright holders to reproduce images.

For Jen, Jinty and Ted
with love

Contents

Preface

'Well, I would say you'd call me an Anglo-Indian because I have a lot of Indian blood in me but way, way back. There was somebody. I don't know the story... but why would I come out like this?'[1]

Anna Kashfi, April 2009

At the time of writing this I know more about Anna Kashfi's family than I do about my own. This is not unusual. Family secrets are not news. Likewise betrayal, estrangement and deception amongst people connected by blood alone are ubiquitous. Families layer their secrets generation upon generation, each obliterating what has gone before and, like snowfall, it alters the landscape. This is a story about how a landscape within a family was altered and why, in the end, the altering destroyed it.

When my mother's father, an avid reader of biographies, died in Lancashire in the 1980s I realised that I had no idea where he was born. Ted was a salesman for Heinz and when we lived with him, while he was between wives, we ate our way through a shed-full of baked beans with pork sausages and steamed chocolate pudding. His second marriage, when he was in his sixties, was to a woman who had lived her entire life in Bolton. Except that it wasn't his second marriage. In between Nettie May (who, for a reason no one knew, Ted called Jinty) and Anne, there was an unhappy interlude with Greta. I didn't know about her. Or perhaps I did and then forgot about it.

Along with thinking that Grandad only had two wives I had assumed that my mother's family were Scottish – mainly because she was born there, as was her mother, Jinty. Ted's background was never discussed – until a friend remarked, after seeing his photograph, that he was obviously Anglo-Indian. It seemed unlikely. Both his parents were white and there had never been any mention of mixed race relationships. Then again, we knew that generations of his family had spent time in India and his skin was darker than ours, his sister Molly's darker still. So to paraphrase Anna Kashfi – why *would* he come out like that?

To understand my family I have to understand Anna Kashfi's family and vice versa. Anna Kashfi was born an O'Callaghan, a name derived from the Gaelic name of O'Ceallanchain meaning 'descendant of Ceallachan'. Ceallach means 'contention' and 'strife'. To understand this story is to understand *contention*. Her journey, from Joan to Anna, O'Callaghan to Kashfi and Kashfi to Brando, involves both the denial and manufacturing of identities, the effects of colonialism upon a generation and a working practice devised by film studios in Los Angeles to create, exploit and promote movie stars known as the 'star machine'[2]. Each of these was a combustible ingredient, much like a family secret. In some, unhappy, combination it could blow people to bits. Add complex family relationships, racial discrimination and a maverick Hollywood superstar to this explosive brew and the story becomes a catastrophe.

All the facts arrive by way of the telling and retelling of Marlon Brando's life. To date there are approximately fifty books about him, all of them perpetuating the myth that Anna Kashfi, his first wife, lied about her background, fooled Brando and betrayed her parents. I say *myth* because I know the truth. That the truth and the stories told on all sides are contradictory, and sometimes downright confusing, obscures the complexity of *why* the stories were told. That's what this book seeks to reveal.

Anna Kashfi herself was both of her time and one of a kind. She witnessed at first hand the last gasp of an Empire, the dying days of Hollywood's golden era and the anti-communist paranoia of 1950s America. As a teenager she was part of an almost forgotten wave of immigrants, a displaced minority returning to a 'home'[3] they had never even seen, and in her early twenties she was subjected to an unprecedented crucifixion by the press on both sides of the Atlantic. By the time she was twenty-five years old she knew betrayal, estrangement and deception better than she knew herself. It was a consequence of her behaviour, no doubt about that. But it was also a gamble she didn't know she was taking. It was the price she paid for marrying the most famous and iconic actor of his generation.

Notes

[1] Anna Kashfi, unpublished recorded interview with author, April 2009.

[2] Jeanine Basinger, *The Star Machine* (Vintage Books, 2009), p. xiii.

[3] Alison Blunt, *Domicile and Diaspora* (Blackwell Publishing, 2005), p.2.

1

The Wedding Day

MR. MARLON BRANDO MARRIED TO INDIAN

Hollywood, Oct. 11 – Mr. Marlon Brando, the actor, to-day married Miss Anna Kashfi, a 23-year-old Indian actress from Darjeeling.

The Times, October 11th 1957

It was unusually warm and Los Angeles reeked of oranges and exhaust fumes on the day that Marlon Brando married his Indian movie starlet girlfriend, Anna Kashfi.[1] And although California is perennially sunny, it's always worth checking the weather on a wedding day. Angelinos did this back then by squinting up at the iconic Hollywood sign to see if their world-famous symbol of opportunity was visible through the smog. This was the decade when four hundred people a day arrived in the city inflating the population of the fastest growing city in America to two and a half million.[2] The addition of more than six hundred thousand cars, or 'smog machines' as some called them, between 1946 and 1953 intensified a toxic vapour now dense enough to conceal mountains, wilt crops, obstruct breathing and propel housewives onto the streets wearing gas masks and waving placards. As Los Angeles juggled its two personalities; 'sunny, hopeful boomtown, and a dire, gritty Smogtown', small victories ensued.[3] Oil companies were urged to cut sulphur emissions, cars were required to use unleaded gas and exhausts were fitted with catalytic converters. It made no difference. As the city grew increasingly out of hand, so did the pungent, obnoxious smog. And, like an ageing ingénue fallen on hard times, the sign itself was also in a state of some disarray. At thirty-four years old, its unprotected wood and sheet metal structure had deteriorated to the point where the first *O* had splintered into a small *u* and the third *O* had fallen away completely – and so, even if the sky was a clear cobalt blue instead of a blanket-coloured brown, looking up to the hills you would see not **HOLLYWOOD** but **HuLLyWO D**. A misspelled misappropriation of what was, in reality, a downtown suburb of the '*Nowhere City*'.[4]

That the City of Angels was still enticing such an enormous influx of people when the advent of television had all but ruined the industry for which it was most famous, is a measure of the potency of dreams. A business which at its peak created four hundred new films every year watched by fifty million Americans a week, still delivered the possibility that you could arrive with a few dollars and an empty suitcase and become an Audrey or a Rock or a Marilyn. If you were a Rita or a Grace, you might also marry a prince, and if you were a Jimmy or a Jerry you might just become wealthy and famous beyond your wildest imaginings.

But it wasn't only the possibility of fame and fortune which sucked people into this city. It wasn't just the sunshine and the palm trees, or the laid-back liquid sound of the West Coast jazz created by Stan Getz and Gerry Mulligan – it was work. Real work. A job and a chance to participate in the American Dream. This opportunity, to live a better, richer, fuller life than you might live elsewhere, was what Los Angeles promised in its 'sunny, hopeful boomtown' years.[5] It assembled more cars than anywhere other than Detroit, made more tyres than any city but Akron, produced more furniture than Grand Rapids, and stitched almost as many clothes as New York. Construction escalated too as houses were built in ever-expanding suburban communities, extending the city boundaries out into the desert valleys.

So what kind of place was it? Back then – a deadly combination of glitter and organised crime. It was a 'front-page town, gritty and eccentric';[6] somewhere that Hollywood's favourite gangster, Mickey Cohen (Bugsy Siegel's right-hand man) signed autographs while *his* bag man Johnny Stompanato had a vile and violent relationship with the much-married film star Lana Turner – who famously said:

> My goal was to have one husband and seven children, but it turned out to be the other way around.[7]

Stompanato was murdered by Turner's daughter, Cheryl Crane, although rumour had it that it was Lana herself who had wielded the knife. It was a corrupt and corrupting town. It was also paranoid, with all that that entailed. People, particularly people in the movie business, were suspicious, fearful and obsessed – with good reason. Although a decade had passed since the infamous Hollywood Ten blacklist was drawn up with the co-operation of the industry chiefs, hundreds of actors, directors and writers believed to have 'Communist sympathies' were still banned from working in the film industry. 'Communist sympathies' was slack terminology for 'subversive' which in turn was an incautious word for 'treacherous'. And although there were members of the Communist Party in the entertainment industry, many of whom had joined as a direct response to the rise of Fascism in Europe in the thirties, most were not. It didn't matter. All were at risk. These were dangerous and life-threatening times for the victims of careless language. This was the era of political persecution at the height of the Cold War, an era of 'cowardly sordid insanity'– and in Los Angeles friends betrayed friends, colleagues betrayed colleagues and no one trusted anyone any more.[8] 'You start out by wanting to keep your friends. In a totalitarian country they want you to betray your friends – and you persuade yourself finally that it is your duty,' Lee J. Cobb mournfully recalled.[9] This was where Anna Kashfi found herself in October 1955, days after her twenty-first birthday. Two weeks later she was dating Marlon Brando, then *the* most famous movie star in the world; this was truly a factory which manufactured dreams.

When Anna met Marlon he was an established presence in Hollywood; a 'player' – the Oscar-winning veteran of eight films and an eye-catching stint in the theatre in New York. His new girlfriend, by contrast, had just spent a month on location in the French Alps making her acting debut as a 'mute Hindu'. 'Optimistic unknown falls for older, established star' was the kind of story that Hollywood turned into box-office gold – and indeed from its earliest incarnation the romance felt managed – at least by the people guiding Kashfi's nascent career. Still, somehow, almost exactly twenty-four months after their first date they found themselves waking up in different parts of Los Angeles on this exceptionally warm October day with a shared future laid out before them.

At Betty Lindermeyer's home in Eagle Rock, an artistic, affluent neighbourhood in north-eastern Los Angeles, preparations for Brando's wedding were well under way. Betty's nephew Marlon, her late sister Dodie's son, was known as Bud to his family and Mar to his friends. To everyone else he was Brando. Nine years earlier he had created the role of Stanley in *A Streetcar Named Desire* and for four successive years was nominated for Best Actor at the Academy Awards, finally winning for *On the Waterfront* in 1954. Now thirty-three, Brando had been a star for eleven years. He grew up in Nebraska with German and Dutch ancestry on one side and Irish and English on the other and was closest to Bessie, his maternal grandmother. It was Bessie who named him Bud. His mother, Dodie, had been an alcoholic. That, and her passion for the theatre, had left a profound and lingering imprint on her children: Bud and his two sisters, Jocelyn (known as Tiddy) and Fran. Fran wasn't at the wedding but Tiddy was, along with their somewhat eccentric Great Aunt June who had recently accompanied Brando to Japan while he worked on *The Teahouse of the August Moon*. Tiddy, an actress whose best-known film role as Glenn Ford's doomed wife in the *The Big Heat* lay four years behind her, was having a difficult time. Blacklisted by the film industry for signing a peace petition (her soon to be ex-husband, the writer Eliot Asinof, was similarly victimised for encouraging the New York Yankees to hire black baseball players), Tiddy now worked mainly in the theatre. She was already very fond of her future sister-in-law, describing Anna as 'beautiful, charming, graceful, winsome'.[10] It was at Tiddy's Thanksgiving Dinner the previous November that the couple had announced their engagement.

Parents were noticeably absent. Dodie had passed away while visiting Betty Lindermeyer three years earlier and Brando's relationship with his father, Marlon Snr., was complicated. On the one hand, Snr., as he was known, ran his son's film company Pennebaker Productions. He also lived in the same apartment block as Kashfi and could therefore be relied upon to monitor her comings and goings. On the other, Brando had apparently banned him from his wedding with the words, 'I'll bury him before I do!'[11] As for Kashfi's family her father had, according to her, recently died in mysterious circumstances in India and of her mother and brother there was no mention. So the bride and groom bulked up with Brando family cousins Mr and Mrs Allen Pardee, and two other couples – both friends of Kashfi's. Peter Berneis, a writer who had adapted Tennessee Williams' *The Glass Menagerie* for the screen, was Brando's best man. His wife Ina, a photographer and sometime roommate of Kashfi's, was matron of honour. The other couple, Kathy and Louis L'Amour (Louis, a pro-lific and popular writer of westerns, was known affectionately as America's Storyteller) had themselves re-cently married – which is possibly why they rallied round the following day when it became clear that Brando had failed to make arrangements for any kind of honeymoon.

Two of Brando's friends, George Glass and Walter Seltzer, played their part in the wedding despite not attending the ceremony. Glass and Seltzer were film publicists now working as executive producers for Pennebaker Productions. Earlier that week they had accompanied the couple on a trip to Riverside, a sprawling city sixty miles east of Los Angeles, to collect the wedding licence. Riverside had been selected to stall the inevitable onslaught of attention from the press. Brando hated journalists or 'assassins with poisoned typewriters ', as he called them.[12] An encounter with Truman Capote, who had plied him with alcohol and who would then publish Brando's uncharacteristic indiscretions in his revelatory profile for the *New Yorker* a month after the wedding, only increased his loathing. Glass and Seltzer had filed for the licence through a court reporter who had agreed to delay making it a matter of public record so that the press would not be alerted. It appears to have been a miserable trip. Brando sat in the front of the car with Glass, while Kashfi was in the back with Seltzer. No-one exchanged a word for the entire hour and a half journey. Brando's henchmen had made no secret of their dislike of their friend's choice of bride. Glass took Snr.'s line that she was a 'blatant gold digger'[13] and Seltzer believed that Brando was suffering from 'a bad case of being an honourable man'.[14] This, presumably, was a snide reference to the fact that a month earlier Kashfi had announced that she was pregnant. Prior to this, although they had been engaged for nearly a year, there were no wedding plans and Brando had continued to have relationships with other women. Kashfi, by turns bewildered and distressed by this, was volatile and there were frequent bust-ups. After one such occasion a passionate reconciliation ensued in Borrego Springs where Brando was filming *The Young Lions*. Kashfi conceived and, a couple of months later, he suggested they get married immediately. She accepted on the understanding that he would now remain faithful to her.

On October 10th, the day before the wedding, a photographer from Paramount Studios arrived at Brando's house in Laurel Canyon View to take some formal pictures of the couple. The Pennebaker Production office was housed within the Paramount Lot, on the corner of Gower Street and Melrose Avenue, and it was Paramount who had given Kashfi her break in *The Mountain* with Spencer Tracy. In fact, they had first met in the studio canteen when Brando was having lunch with Eva Marie Saint, his co-star from *On the Waterfront*. But the choice of photographer was no act of sentimental loyalty on Brando's part – he was a gun for hire and Kashfi, by now, was under contract to MGM. Indeed, an indication of the decline of the studio-controlled star system was that one of its most successful stars ran his own independent company while working for each of the major studios in turn. So why the official wedding photographs? The most likely explanation is that Brando was simply seeking to control the publicity. The pictures would be released after the ceremony had taken place and by the time they were front page news, the couple would have left town. A week later, after the story had died down, they would return and continue living the relatively low-profile existence which Brando was intent on preserving. That, at least, was the plan.

And then, of course, there was the pregnancy. Still an enormous scandal in conservative, post-war America; 'abortion was unthinkable, illegitimacy unbearable, marriage inevitable'.[15] Weddings of the shotgun variety were useful, with 'premature' births a few months later solving the problem. *Brando's July Baby* would indeed be the headline in the *Daily Mirror* a month after their October wedding, while in reality the child was born on 11th May 1958 (exactly seven months after the ceremony – and nine months since the reconciliation in Borrego Springs in August 1957). No matter, the studios would go to just about any lengths to protect their investments. Quashing any evidence of what might be regarded as immoral behaviour, they made whatever arrangements were necessary swiftly and discreetly.

Looking at the photographs, there is an unsettling severity about the bride and groom. One shows them against a backdrop of two palm trees in Brando's garden overlooking the canyon. Kashfi, barefoot and dressed in a white sari, stands with one arm clasped through Brando's and the other stretched across her waist. A platinum-blonde Brando, his hair bleached for his role as a German officer in *The Young Lions*, stares at the camera. Both are unsmiling and their expressions inscrutable. Serious, certainly, but there is something else. The complexity of their relationship, characterised as it is by infidelity, suspicion and a magnetic physical attraction, is what lies beneath. In another photograph, this one taken inside the house, neither looks at the camera. Brando has his hands in his pockets while Kashfi, eyes slightly glazed, holds hers protectively over her stomach.

9

They spent the night before the wedding apart – that much we know and it's hardly unusual. Accounts differ about Brando's behaviour the following morning. Alice Marchak, Brando's assistant, said that when she was summoned to his house along with his agent Jay Kanter, he was in bed with an unnamed woman. He announced, to their surprise, he was getting married but at one o'clock was still at home searching for shoes with just half an hour to go before the ceremony. Another report places him in Pasadena, dressed in an opera cloak and a homburg hat, buying a wedding ring before driving himself to his Aunt Betty's.[16] Meanwhile, Kashfi, dressed in either a pale sea-green (or pink – reports vary) sari embroidered in gold, and wearing red shoes, asked Louis L'Amour to stop the car en route to Eagle Rock because she was having a 'premonition – an eerie feeling – that I shouldn't be doing this'. Louis advised her that there was an hour to go and she could still back out if she wanted to.[17]

At Betty Lindermeyer's house, the wedding party assembled. Peter and Ina Berneis arrived followed by the appropriately named L'Amours with Kashfi, who had evidently overcome her reservations. Brando, in a dark blue suit and sporting the opera cloak, was next. The cloak proved troublesome, roaming dangerously across chairs, lamps and potted plants, prompting his soon-to-be wife to snap irritably 'For Chrissake Marlon, take off that damn cape'. Last to arrive was the Reverend J. Walter Fiscus from the Little Brown Church of the Valley in North Hollywood; twenty years later Kashfi would remember him as a 'large, florid man with protruding incisors'. She had originally wanted a Buddhist ritual and Brando a Zen wedding; they compromised on an Episcopalian service – hence the florid Fiscus. After the Reverend's entrance, perhaps in an attempt to assert her status, the bride-to-be interrupted proceedings and demanded a bunch of Madonna lilies. She may or may not have known or cared that when used as a bridal bouquet lilies are a symbol of fertility; still her request infuriated Brando. Various florists were contacted in an attempt to placate the jittery Kashfi, but to no avail. Eventually, someone got Paramount involved and they began searching for Madonna lilies in other cities. Hours passed, the champagne was opened and the desultory wedding party limped along. By the time the bouquet was finally flown in from San Francisco, Kashfi described herself as 'tipsy enough to have said "I do" to a baboon'.[18]

Since no arrangements had been made for a honeymoon, after leaving Aunt Betty's the most famous actor in the world and his new wife drove around Los Angeles for an hour in his Thunderbird convertible while they decided what to do. Kashfi, who had dreamed of a cruise or a tour of European capitals, could not have been pleased when eventually Brando phoned his agent and asked for suggestions as to where they might spend their wedding night. Jay Kanter was one of the few people he trusted implicitly. When Brando moved to the West Coast, the new mailroom boy at MCA, then the largest talent agency in the world, chauffeured him about. At the end of his first week, when asked which agent he wanted to represent him, Brando said 'the kid who's been driving me around'.[19] Kanter was speedily promoted – a sign of just how valuable a property Brando already was. Affable, decent and well-versed in the actor's number one requirement of loyalty, he immediately offered to vacate his house in Beverly Hills so that the newlyweds could stay there. It wasn't a night to remember. 'There was no sex,' according to Kashfi. 'There was mostly concern from Marlon about what Jay and his wife were saying about me.'[20]

On Saturday October 12th the couple woke up to newspaper reports of the marriage of 'Hollywood's most eligible and sought after bachelor'. 'Secretive Brando' was said to have caught the film world 'way off guard'.[21] Everything was going according to plan – apart from the problem of where to head next. After breakfast they took to the streets again, driving about aimlessly like a couple of rich kids with no particular place to go. Finally, in desperation, Kashfi phoned the L'Amours, now back home on their ranch just outside Palm Springs and asked if they could spend the honeymoon with them. Whether they actually made it that far – together or separately – is a matter of dispute. Kashfi herself maintained that she and Kathy spent the week cleaning the house while her new husband and Louis shot tin cans in the yard with a .38 revolver. She said that the two couples watched television and picked oranges together and that, less charmingly, Brando entertained them at breakfast by extinguishing cigarettes on the back of his hand.[22] Alice Marchak disagreed. According to her, Brando holed up with Seltzer and Glass while they worked out what to do next – and no one knew where Kashfi was.[23]

The roots of the discrepancy lay in the incident which had blown the marriage apart within hours of the service.

While the American papers, as anticipated, had run the story about Marlon Brando's surprise wedding, the British press took advantage of the time difference and investigated the background of the little-known Kashfi. Within hours the *Times* announcement, *Brando Married to Indian*, was rapidly replaced around the world by the infinitely more newsworthy headline; *Britisher Says Brando's Bride Ex-Butcher Girl*.[24] This was then picked up by the American syndicated press and made the front page news across the United States in every local paper from *The Oneonta Star* (*Welsh Mother Says Brando's Bride is Hers, Not Indian*) to *The Independent Star-News* (*Brando's Indian Bride Held an O'Callaghan*) as well as bigger beasts like the iconic *New York Times* (*Kashfi Called Welsh*). The claim, made by a 'Welsh factory worker' living in Cardiff, changed everything for Kashfi. William O'Callaghan declared that the woman known in Hollywood as India's answer to Grace Kelly was in fact his daughter, a former butcher's assistant named Joan O'Callaghan. To make matters worse, 'Mr. O'Callaghan's English wife' insisted 'there is no Indian blood in my family or my husband's family'.[25] It's hard to imagine a greater contrast of emotions for Kashfi within a twenty-four-hour period – from marrying a famous film star to enduring a brutalising onslaught from the world's press. Nothing in this naive young woman's background, whether Welsh or Indian, had prepared her for this. Two years in Los Angeles, almost twelve months of which had been spent in an isolation ward as she recovered from TB, certainly didn't. She was, to use modern parlance, hung out to dry. The papers implied that she was a liar and Brando a fool – a humiliation for which he never forgave her. The firestorm which engulfed the couple was to have terrible consequences.

Anna Kashfi was both of her time and one of a kind – a part of history and yet also extinguished from it.

Years later, thinking about this moment in her life – the moment when she had everything and then had nothing – Kashfi said:

Shouldn't I be dead or something, or in a rest home with my mind gone?[26]

Notes

[1] Jack Smith quoting H.L. Mencken on his first visit to Los Angeles in 'A Teflon Metropolis Where No Nicknames Stick', *The Los Angeles Times*, 12 October 1989.

[2] Kevin Starr, *Los Angeles: Portrait of a City*, (Taschen, 2009), p. 306.

[3] Chip Jacobs & William J. Kelly, *Smogtown: The Lung-Burning History of Pollution in Los Angeles*, (The Overlook Press, 2008), p. 162.

[4] Jack Smith, *The Los Angeles Times*, 12 October 1989.

[5] Chip Jacobs & William J. Kelly, *Smogtown: The Lung-Burning History of Pollution in Los Angeles*, p. 41.

[6] Kevin Starr, *Los Angeles: Portrait of a City*, p. 305.

[7] James Robert Parish, *The Hollywood Book of Extravagance: The Totally Infamous, Mostly Disastrous, and Always Compelling Excesses of America's Film and TV Idols*, (John Wiley & Sons, 2011), p. 249.

[8] Michael Freedland, *Witch-Hunt in Hollywood: McCarthyism's War on Tinseltown*, (JR Books, 2009), p.4.

[9] Sam Kashner & Jennifer MacNair, *The Bad and the Beautiful: Hollywood in the Fifties*, (Norton, 2003) p. 77.

[10] Peter Manso, *Brando*, (Weidenfeld & Nicolson, 1994), p. 420.

[11] Charles Higham, *Brando: The Unauthorized Biography*, (New American Library, 1987), p. 190.

[12] Anna Kashfi & E.P. Stein, *Brando for Breakfast*, (Crown Publishers, 1979), p. 101.

[13] Peter Manso, *Brando*, p. 449.

[14] Ibid., p. 461.

[15] Stefan Kanfer, *Somebody: The Reckless Life and Remarkable Career of Marlon Brando*, (Faber and Faber, 2008), p. 157.

[16] Charles Higham, *Brando: The Unauthorized Biography*, p. 190.

[17] Anna Kashfi, *Brando for Breakfast*, p. 108.

[18] Ibid., p. 109.

[19] Stefan Kanfer, *Somebody: The Reckless Life and Remarkable Career of Marlon Brando*, p. 93.

[20] Peter Manso, *Brando*, p.462.

[21] *San Mateo Times*, 12 October 1957.

[22] Anna Kasfhi, *Brando for Breakfast*, p. 111.

[23] Alice Marchak, *Me and Marlon*, (BookMasters, 2008), p. 20.

[24] *The Daily Review*, 12 October 1957.

[25] *The New York Times*, 13 October 1957.

[26] Sarah Broughton, 'Unpublished Recorded Interviews with Anna Kashfi', April 2009.

2

A Passage to England

Anglo-Indians are quintessentially the children of colonialism. They are descendants of the initial offspring of unions – formal and casual – involving British and other European men on the one side, and, on the other, local 'Indian' as well as other women who – especially in the context of south India – came under the inclusive if vague category of 'Portuguese'. Anglo-Indians are thus the inheritors of a diversity of national, ethnic and caste backgrounds. Like other similarly constituted hybrid groups in a colonial context, they were subject to a frequently shifting set of criteria that allowed them privilege at certain historical moments and pointedly excluded them at others.[1]

Lionel Caplan, *Children of Colonialism: Anglo-Indians in a Postcolonial World*

On 13th September 1948 a ship named the S.S. Ranchi, with nine hundred and fifty 'tourist class' passengers, arrived at Tilbury Docks, twenty-five miles downstream from London Bridge. Three months earlier, when the Empire Windrush had delivered Jamaican immigrants in search of a new life in Britain to the same dockside, the *Daily Express* ran an ominous headline: '*450 arrive – Get pep talk: "Things will not be easy"*.'[2] There was no such fanfare for the Ranchi, no cameras to record the newcomers as they slipped into the port – but the newspapers could have run more or less the same headlines.

Twenty-three years old and on her first round trip since being refitted after war duties the Ranchi was now a functional transport carrier rather than the luxury liner she had once been. Originally commissioned by the Peninsular & Oriental Steam Navigation Company (P&O) for the London to Bombay mail service and named after the capital city of Jharkhand state in Eastern India, she was built in Newcastle alongside her three sister ships, the Ranpura, the Rawalpindi and the Rajputana. Alongside her postal duties, the Ranchi, an 'R' class liner (so called because they pioneered the new refrigerated spaces for cargo of fish and fruit), cruised with five hundred and eighty-seven first and second class passengers until the golden years of Ocean travel ended abruptly with the advent of World War Two. The Ranchi was requisitioned for wartime service in August 1939 and used initially as an armed merchant cruiser and then as a troopship. After the war she was returned to P&O and by the time she sailed out of Bombay, in August 1948, she had reinvented herself again – this time as a 'migrant carrier'.[3] Times had changed and the days of first, second, third class and steerage with separate accommodation for ayahs and maids and segregated quarters for crew were gone. On migrant carriers everyone travelled together in one classless space.

Although in her new role the Ranchi was supposed to convey 'Ten Pound Poms'[4] taking advantage of the 'Populate or Perish' policy created by the Australian

Government in 1945, the voyage which was to end in Tilbury Docks in September 1948 was different. It was an exodus, of sorts, of people from the recently divided nation of India to England – yet the passengers, for the most part, had British or Irish sounding names. There were Palmers and Woods, O'Neils and O'Connells. A clue as to who they were might be found in their occupations which ranged from light house keepers to civil engineers to chemists and missionaries, stenographers and doctors. Not so easy to work out were the married women who were labelled either 'H.D.' (Home Duties) or 'Wife' in the Occupation column.

Children accompanied their parents and on this voyage there were two who would become extremely famous. Both would change their names. Both would tell their story, or a story, in different ways over the years to come. Their mothers, Mrs Phoebe Melinda O'Callaghan and Mrs Dorothy Marie Webb, were listed as 'H.D.' and their fathers, Mr William O'Callaghan and Mr Rodger Webb, were listed as 'Rly. Official' and 'Commercial Asst.' respectively. 'Rly. Official' in William's case meant Head Train Controller on the Bengal Nagpur Railway, while Rodger's 'Commercial Asst.' was a fleeting description of someone who had worked his way up from steward to manager at Kellner & Co – a large firm which looked after the catering for several of the railway lines including the East Indian Railway. The O'Callaghans and the Webbs were railway people. By the time they sailed away from India on the 24th August 1948, twelve months and ten days had passed since the Indian Independence Act was implemented. It was drawn up by Labour Prime Minister

Clement Attlee and Lord Louis Mountbatten, Governor General of India, and uncle of Philip the soon-to-be husband of Princess Elizabeth. The Act split British India into two separate countries: Pakistan and India. During that year the increasing violence, the assassination of Gandhi and the abruptly precarious nature of their jobs hastened both families' departures. They were leaving a country that had been good to them, but was now unfamiliar, in search of one they had never set foot in but hoped would make them welcome. It was, after all, the place Anglo-Indians called 'home'.[5]

The exodus of Anglo-Indians following Indian Independence was fuelled in part by the British Nationality Act of 1948. This guaranteed right of repatriation to Britain to all white Britons who had served in the colonial dominions prior to decolonisation became immeasurably significant to the Anglo-Indian community living in India as they witnessed the changing landscape of the only world they knew. Under Section 12 of the Act people who were direct descendants of those born or naturalised in the United Kingdom could apply for a passport – as long as they could provide documentary proof of their ancestor's place of birth. But, as Rochelle Almeida points out in *Britain's Anglo-Indians*, many members of the community would have been 'unable to prove their fathers' or grandfathers' birthplace in the United Kingdom'.[6] Consequently, many second or third generation Anglo-Indians who were born in India had to apply to be registered as 'Citizens of the United Kingdom and Colonies' – creating a feeling of resentment and bewilderment for people who believed they shouldn't have to make a formal claim to what was theirs by right already. Ian R. G. Spencer provides definitive evidence that British officials were inclined to make it difficult for Anglo-Indians to legally enter Britain following Indian Independence. In his analysis of post-war British immigration policy, Spencer maintains that:

> Officials were totally unsympathetic to the plight of Anglo-Indians and Anglo-Pakistanis whose privileged position under the Raj in, for example, the railway and postal services, was coming under pressure and who were, therefore, looking for alternative sources of employment. Officials did not think that they would be useful in Britain and hence: 'we should not be displeased to see Anglo-Indians experiencing difficulty in obtaining travel documents to emigrate from India'.[7]

This hostile attitude remained long in the memory as Rochelle Almeida highlighted in an interview with an 83-year-old Anglo-Indian woman who emigrated to Britain in 1952:

> Considering how hostile the officials were to us and how difficult they made it to leave India and to settle in this country, you'd think we were a bunch of thugs rather than hard-working, morally upright Christian men and women who had served the Empire well and only wished to be rewarded for our loyalty.[8]

This then was the climate in which the O'Callaghan family left India. Their journey would take them from Bombay to Aden for a four-hour stop and then on through the Red Sea towards the Suez Canal and a six-hour stretch in Egypt's Port Said before beginning the final leg of the journey across the Mediterranean Sea to Britain. Why the Port Said stopover? Spencer suggests there were several loopholes by which people that may have experienced problems in obtaining British passports could enter the United Kingdom. One was by forged passports and another was by travelling first from the Indian sub-continent to a second country from which you could then, apparently, proceed without hindrance to Britain. Spencer maintained that 'from those second countries prospective immigrants could embark for the United Kingdom without fear of difficulties,' because the authorities were less scrupulous about approving travel to the Holy Places.[9]

Eleven days after leaving Port Said, the passengers disembarked at six a.m. on a chilly September morning at Tilbury Docks. In 1948 Tilbury was the main British port for the importation of paper – which was in short supply back in those post-war days. It wasn't the only commodity that was scarce – meat, clothes, petrol and sugar were still rationed – and Britain itself was almost bankrupt. It was nonetheless a historic time to be arriving in the capital city – London had recently hosted the first summer Olympics since the notorious Berlin Games of 1936, while the new, much heralded cornerstone of the Labour Government's implementation of the Beveridge Report, the National Health Service, had been in operation for a little over two months. Not only that – as luck would have it, they had managed to avoid one of the worst winters in living memory. By the time of the next record-breaking freeze some fifteen years later, life would have changed immeasurably for Joan O'Callaghan.

No matter – when they came ashore the climate must still have been a nasty shock for the travellers who had spent their entire lives in India. Life began amidst heavy rain and gales aboard the cross-river ferry which took passengers from the Ranchi to the Tilbury Landing Stage – a large, elegant pavilion-like structure jutting over the river which bore silent witness to the humankind which flowed through it. From there they stepped into the cathe-dralesque Baggage Hall. Designed by Sir Edwin Cooper, an architect said to be responsible for more buildings in the City of London than Sir Christopher Wren, it handled comings and goings from all over the world.

From the Baggage Hall it was a short walk across bridges to the Tilbury Riverside station and then a forty-five minute train journey into central London. Where *were* these hundreds of people – the H.Ds, the Motor Drivers and the Nurses – going? The Ranchi's passenger list hints at a range of narratives through the barest of facts. There are names, occupations and ages of passengers, Country of Last Permanent Residence and Country of Intended Future Permanent Residence. The Proposed Addresses column throws up a haphazard list of destinations includ-ing Harpenden, Rhyl, Hartlepool and Bath. India House in Aldwych, home of the Indian High Commission, is a 'care of' address given by many. Cordon (a misspelling of Gordon perhaps?) O'Neill, a poultry farmer, is on his way to Castle View, Eye Hill in Dudley; or perhaps that is also an error – there was an *Eve* Hill in Dudley in the 1940s. The Webb family listed Windborough Road in Carshalton as their 'Proposed Address in the United Kingdom' while the O'Callaghans registered Thornton Road in Ilford, then a thriving borough north-east of London best known for the photographic company founded there in 1879, as theirs.[10]

It's not known if the O'Callaghan family spent any time in Ilford. There was always a different destination in mind and, soon after arriving in Britain, they travelled some one hundred and fifty miles across England and into Wales to the seaside village of Ogmore-by-Sea. This was where they spent the autumn and winter of 1948 and 1949 before moving twenty miles east into the city of Cardiff. Joan O'Callaghan, when asked why her parents had chosen Ogmore-by-Sea – or how they had even known of its existence – said that her mother had met a soldier during the war who had come from there.[11] She liked him and when they came to make their plans of where they might settle when they decided to go 'home', Ogmore-by-Sea must have seemed as good a place as anywhere else. And so the family from India settled in south Wales.

Joan O'Callaghan changed her name when she became an actress in 1955. In her first role, in the film *The Mountain*, she has a non-speaking part as a Hindu girl and is credited as Anna Kashfi. Her story, famous though it briefly and sensationally was, is less well documented. The narrators, William, Phoebe and Joan herself, all proved themselves to be unreliable. Later others further obfuscated until who knew *what* the truth really was? There are records but they are really just glimpses into a world that is seldom explored – a mirror to all of us about the complicated story of ourselves.

Carshalton, where the Webb family first settled, is where I was born. My maternal grandfather's birthplace was Bangalore, known as the 'Garden City' of India.[12] My mother, exactly two months older than Joan O'Callaghan, travelled to India from Scotland (where her mother had been sent home to give birth to her) when she was a few weeks old. Her grandfather and great uncle were also railway people – Permanent Way Inspectors who looked after the track. In the late 1930s most of the family left India and never returned. There my tenuous connection with this story mostly ends. Except that we too never discussed who we were or the colour of my grandfather's skin.

We do not know if the O'Callaghan and Webb families met during their five weeks at sea – there were, after all, almost a thousand people on board. As I have said, both families were railway people: the O'Callaghans from Adra in West Bengal and the Webbs in Howrah, a large industrial city also in West Bengal. Joan O'Callaghan was the oldest of the children at nearly fifteen and her brother, Bosco, celebrated his twelfth birthday on board the Ranchi. Harry Webb, almost eight, was travelling with his younger sisters, Donna and Jacqui. Leaving the Baggage Hall at Tilbury Docks, the two families' stories diverge. Their shared past was a life in India lived under the British Raj and this journey to a new world on the same ship. What became of the Webb family is well documented, although how they left the port itself is disputed. Harry Webb was to tell the story that his father hired a taxi to Carshalton with his last five pounds, but his mother maintained that they were picked up by a private car from Tilbury and spent their first few days in England with her mother's aunt who lived somewhere in south-east London. Whenever it was that the Webbs arrived at Carshalton Station what lay ahead of them was a daunting prospect. Their new home was a three-bedroomed semi-detached house they would share with Dorothy Marie's mother, her step-father, and their seven children, who had already made the journey from India some months earlier. Harry recalled the early days in England sixty years later:

> We were destitute. My father sold everything he had in India to raise enough money for our passage, but because the flat we lived in belonged to the company, he had very little to sell. We arrived in Britain with £5. That was it. Worse, my father couldn't find work. He was sixteen years older than my mother. So already in his forties; it was just after the War, rationing was still in place and there was very little work to be had, particularly for someone of his age.[13]

For thirteen months fourteen people crammed themselves into the semi and lived cheek by jowl; 'We were sleeping all over the place,' remembered one of the fourteen, Vincent Dickson.[14] The situation was intolerable and so the Webbs moved in with Rodger's sister in Waltham Cross on the other side of London hoping to get onto the council house waiting list. Rodger's sister and her husband Ernest had two sons, with scarcely more space than the Dicksons had had, and tensions rose as the Webbs found themselves again living in one small room. Finally in April

1951, and now with four children, Rodger and Dorothy moved into a council house in Cheshunt. Harry Webb, almost eight years old when he arrived in Britain, changed his name ten years later to Cliff Richard when singing with his first band *The Drifters*.

Notes

[1] Lionel Caplan, *Children of Colonialism: Anglo-Indians in a Post-colonial World,* (Berg, 2001), p.51.

[2] *Daily Express*, 22 June 1948.

[3] P&O Heritage, Ship Fact Sheet http://www.poheritage.com/upload/Mimsy/Media/factsheet/94342RANCHI-1925pdf.pdf.

[4] Immigration Museum, Melbourne, Australia. https://museumvictoria.com.au/immigrationmuseum/discoverycentre/your-questions/ten-pound-poms/

[5] Lionel Caplan, *Children of Colonialism*, p.98.

[6] Rochelle Almeida, *Britain's Anglo-Indians: The Invisibility of Assimilation,* (Lexington Books, 2017), p.27.

[7] Ian R. G. Spencer, *British Immigration Policy Since 1939: The Making of Multi-Racial Britain,* (Routledge, 1997), p. 26.

[8] Rochelle Almeida, *Britain's Anglo-Indians: The Invisibility of Assimilation,* pp. 22-23.

[9] Ian R. G. Spencer, *British Immigration Policy Since 1939: The Making of Multi-Racial Britain,* p. 28.

[10] The Ranchi's passenger list, Ancestry United Kingdom: Incoming Passenger Lists.

[11] Sarah Broughton, 'Unpublished Recorded Interviews with Anna Kashfi', April 2009.

[12] David Abram, *The Rough Guide to India,* |(Rough Guides, 2005), p. 1282.

[13] Cliff Richard, *My Life, My Way*, (Headline Review, 2008), p.7.

[14] Steve Turner, *Cliff Richard: The Biography*, (Lion, 1998), p. 49.

3

Brando's Bride: Welsh Or Injun?[1]

KASHFI CALLED WELSH

Brando's Indian Bride Held Daughter of Cardiff Man

CARDIFF, Wales, October 12th 1957

A Welsh factory worker, William Patrick O'Callaghan, said tonight that Anna Kashfi, bride of Marlon Brando, was his 23-year-old daughter Joan. The news of Miss Kashfi's marriage yesterday to the Hollywood star created a stir here. The actress went to Hollywood a little more than a year ago to complete scenes for 'The Mountain,' in which she appeared with Spencer Tracy. Mr. O'Callaghan said his daughter, a former model, took the name Anna Kashfi for the film. He added that she had been born in Darjeeling, India, where he was a traffic superintendent for the Indian State Railways. The report could not be confirmed in Hollywood yesterday afternoon. Mr. O'Callaghan's English wife told newsmen 'there is no Indian blood in my family or my husband's family'. In Hollywood, Edward Dmytryk, director, who gave the young woman her first important role in 'The Mountain,' said he knew her real name was Irish, 'but I assumed she was Anglo-Indian.'[2]

The New York Times

On Monday 14th October 1957, following a weekend of global uproar about the identity of Marlon Brando's new wife, the *Tucson Daily Citizen* posed the following question for its readers: *Who is Brando's Bride?* The answer made its way across geographical borders from Ireland to Wales, skittered past France and ricocheted back and forth to England. Anywhere, in fact, other than the nationality 'Brando's Indian Bride' claimed for herself.[3] Since then the woman who had, apparently, 'arrived in Hollywood deliberately to seduce him [Brando] and form a relationship with him, having already heard of his penchant for liking exotic women' has had a generic, yet essentially British, nationality fashioned for her.[4] Newspaper articles published after the wedding formed the basis for Kashfi's reputation for the next half century – and thus she is variously described by Brando's biographers as being:

> Of Welsh parentage, she had been born in India and educated there in a convent school.[5]

> She was the daughter of a dark-skinned Frenchwoman and an English railroad worker currently living in Wales.[6]

> Joanna O'Callaghan, a Welsh girl from Cardiff with rather tenuous claims to an Indian mystique.[7]

And the belief that she had fictionalised her Indian background was unanimous:

> the Brandos were invited everywhere, because just about every woman in town wanted to see this mysterious 'Indian' Marlon had married.[8]

> She had been raised in India, but she isn't Indian at all.[9]

One of Marlon's detectives concluded in his report that Kashfi 'was about as Indian as Queen Elizabeth of England.'[10]

The inconsistencies between the various stories, not to mention Kashfi's appearance coupled with the fact that she herself altered her tale from time to time, might have made an astute biographer at least sound a note of caution. But still, to date, no one has viewed this in the context of the circumstances – that Los Angeles was a city full of unreliable narrators and that the very business of film was the business of fiction. Or as Bertolt Brecht, put it: 'Every morning to earn my bread, I go to the market where lies are bought'.[11] Howard Strickling, the formidable Head of Publicity at MGM Studios and widely known within the industry as 'the fixer', was a hawker of unreliable narratives – probably the best in the business.[12] If they got into trouble stars were told: 'Don't call the police. Don't call the hospital. Don't call your lawyer. Call Howard.'[13] So, to an extent, Kashfi's fate was in Strickling's hands. Now though, for once, rather than fictionalising the story, he told the truth and admitted that the studio had been issuing pay cheques to Kashfi in the name of 'Johanna O'Callaghan'. He was, however, quick to add that he 'remained in the dark as to whether she was the daughter of a factory worker in Cardiff, Wales'.[14] He wouldn't confirm the reports and added dismissively, 'I'll check them Monday'. For Strickling Kashfi would have been the smallest of fry, despite the Brando connection. He had spent the previous half-century of his working life protecting MGM's biggest assets, stars like Clark

Gable and Greta Garbo, who were worth millions to the studio. If fans knew, for instance, that Gable had fathered an illegitimate child or that Garbo was known to be an 'active bisexual' the results could be disastrous: losing the asset could doom a studio – which is why Strickling *fixed things*.[15]

Kashfi's circumstances, despite her abrupt marriage to Brando, were the same as any other actor working for the star machine at that time. Every major film studio – the 'Big Five' as they were known (MGM, Paramount, Warner Bros, Fox and RKO) – created a 'fake biography' for every actor who was under contract.[16] It was the publicity department's job to manufacture a back-story about the (potential) star. According to film historian Jeanine Basinger this was 'an imaginative, somewhat whimsical, often hilarious, and definitely ripe for satire process.' Sometimes the back-story was based largely on the truth and sometimes it strayed very far from it. Sometimes an actual identity transplant took place. This happened without exception with Jewish actors. Otto Friedrich, author of the acclaimed *City of Nets*: *A Portrait of Hollywood in the 1940's*, believes that the Mayers and Warners and Goldwyns (the original heads of the biggest studios) yearned for assimilation, and 'a suppression or even a symbolic denial of all Jewishness', led to their insistence on changing names:

> In a way, the simplest and most insignificant of evasions – even a Julia Turner was renamed Lana, after all – and yet there was something profoundly degrading in the unwritten rule that no star could have a Jewish name.[17]

Kirk Douglas, Jerry Lewis and Karl Malden all had a change of name and a glossing over of their Jewish backgrounds. But sometimes there were different ethnic reasons. Twenty years before Anna Kashfi was accused of fictionalising her Indian identity, part Spanish, part Irish-American Margarita Carmen Cansino was transformed into the more American-sounding Rita Hayworth. Although Cansino had played an Egyptian, an Argentinian and a Russian in her early career, when she signed with Columbia Studios her 'fake biography' decreed she adopt her mother's maiden name (Hayworth) and transform her appearance from ethnic-looking beauty into an all-American glamour girl through make-up, hair colour and an electrolysis treatment which lifted her hairline.

Not everyone altered their appearance – but the name change was fairly ubiquitous, Jewish or not. Clifton Webb (aka Webb Parmalee Hollenbeck) and Rock Hudson (aka Roy Schere Jr) were just two of the male box office draws who were renamed for the benefit of a movie-going audience. Amongst the women Tula Ellice Finklea became Cyd Charisse, Constance Ockleman adopted the more seductive sounding Veronica Lake and a matching hair style, and Frances Ethel Gumm from Grand Rapids, Minnesota, transformed herself into Judy Garland. Names were changed to fit the persona the Studio was fashioning for the star; Marion Michael Morrison is perhaps the most famous example – today he lives on as John Wayne and is best known for his tough guy cowboy roles. When the Irish-sounding Joan O'Callaghan was cast as 'Hindu Girl' opposite Spencer Tracy in her first film *The Mountain*, her name was changed to Anna Kashfi. Joan O'Callaghan, who was living in London at the time, shared a flat with an agent's assistant, Glynn Mortimer. According to the American magazine *Parade*, Mortimer, who had reputedly passed on the information about the casting call for a Hindu actress to her friend Joan, told them:

> I'm the one who gave her the name Anna Kashfi. Kashfi was the name of a dear friend of mine. Joan picked the name Anna from Joanna, which she apparently had used from time to time.[18]

On her 21st birthday Anna Kashfi arrived in New York en route to Los Angeles to finish work on *The Mountain*. Kashfi, the first Indian actress to be signed in Hollywood, was marketed to American movie fans as 'the Grace Kelly of India'.[19] Unlike the mixed-race actress Merle Oberon, who went to extraordinarily painful lengths to be accepted as a white woman from Tasmania, Kashfi embraced her new image. Her first 'star biography', also known as a 'studio bio', didn't list her parents' names and the snippets that appear in the press refer to her younger brother, Bosco (who was indeed her younger brother – the truth occasionally proving useful) and father 'Devi Kashfi'. Kashfi, or 'East Indian beauty' as she was usually labelled, was on the map.[20] Just as nobody referred to John as Marion any more, Anna was now Anna and never Joan.

By the time of her marriage to Brando, Kashfi was beginning to establish herself. After two years in Los Angeles she had completed three films, not many by industry standards, but there had also been a lengthy stay in hospital recovering from TB. She had a seven-year contract with the mighty MGM studios. She was just twenty-three years old and she was pregnant. She had a lot to lose. When journalists started knocking on William O'Callaghan's front door in Cardiff, headlines like *Brand's Bride Welsh or Injun?*;[21] *Hollywood Wallows in Mystery of Real Race of Brando's Bride*;[22] *Brando's "Indian Wife" May Turn Out Welsh*;[23] *Mrs Brando's Brogue Is Showing, 'Tis Said*;[24] all speculated on the legitimacy of his astonishing declaration. When O'Callaghan temporarily retreated to his bed, having succumbed to the Asian flu epidemic sweeping the country, it was left to Phoebe O'Callaghan to speak her mind. The sudden besieging of their modest semi-detached house in a quiet suburb just north of the city centre must have been shocking for the couple. 'Is Anna disowning us?' she asked, seemingly bewildered by what was happening.[25] 'I feel very angry – and very sad,'[26] she told the journalists camped outside her front door in Newfoundland Road, only to find her obvious distress translated into a series of mawkish headlines: *Brando Mother-in-Law Cries for Lost 'Anna'*;[27] *Brando Bride's Mother Weeps*;[28] *Come Back, Joanna, We Still Love You.*[29] While the O'Callaghans' very personal anguish was being played out in newsprint, Edward Dmytryk, director of *The Mountain*, but better known as one of the 'Hollywood Ten', stepped forward to say he knew 'Kashfi's real name was Irish but assumed she was Anglo-Indian'.[30] After which, William O'Callaghan reappeared, possibly panicked, to declare 'she's our daughter, and both me and the missus were born in London' and, later, 'I can assure you that she is absolutely English and has no Indian blood in her whatsoever.' These comments were widely reported in newspapers across Britain and the United States including the *Los Angeles Examiner*. The O'Callaghans' robust insistence on their Englishness meant that Anna/Joan would be forever labelled as, at best, a fantasist and at worst, 'totally schizy and obviously lying.'[31]

Faced with the destruction of the life she had created, Kashfi fought back. She had lied on her Marriage License and, perhaps in order to protect herself from the consequences of that, now she lied again. Responding to contradictory reports in the press she released a statement; 'Brando's All-Indian Bride Explains Her Name':

> I was born in Calcutta to my Indian parents, Devi Kashfi, a civil engineer and architect and Selma Ghose on Sept. 30th 1934. We moved to Darjeeling shortly thereafter. I attended St. Helena's Covent in Kurseong, India until I was 17. When I was 16 my mother remarried William Patrick O'Callaghan. I acquired their name and used it as my legal name on my first trip to England in 1952. I lived for a short time with my mother in Cardiff and studied English at St. Joseph's Convent School. I returned to India briefly and then went back to London. Two years ago I came to this country as a non-immigrant visitor on a petition by Loew's Inc. On this petition as on my marriage license my parents are listed as Devi Kashfi and Selma Ghose, both Indian. I was advised of my father's death during the last Labor Day weekend. I reiterate, my mother, now married to O'Callaghan and a British citizen, is Indian.[32]

It isn't difficult to discern the hand of Howard Strickling at work here. However, it's clear that Kashfi *must* have supplied the entirely fictional names of her birth parents – Selma Ghose and Devi Kashfi. Ghose was the name of the family who owned the Indian scarf shop where she had worked in London's Piccadilly Circus and we know from Glynn Mortimer's interview with *Parade* that she suggested Kashfi. No wonder Phoebe O'Callaghan was distraught – her only daughter refused to recognise her existence. At least William gets a cursory parental foot in the door with the grudging 'stepfather' acknowledgement. More to the point – Kashfi had given *Indian* names to her parents (as well as placing them out of wedlock). It must have felt like a cruel rejection for William and Phoebe O'Callaghan.

The Kashfi scandal had been front page news for five days now and showed no sign of disappearing. While Brando wasn't under contract to MGM at that time, Kashfi was less than halfway through her seven-year deal. The studio stood by her: 'Anna always maintained she was Anglo-Indian... William O'Callaghan was only her step-father.'[33] Nonetheless, it was damage limitation time. The press had detected that perhaps something was amiss. There are numerous sly references to Phoebe O'Callaghan's colouring which hint that perhaps the story was not as straightforward as it seemed. And, at the centre of the drama was the phenomenally famous, publicity-hating Marlon Brando. This was a story that sold newspapers. The strange revelation, again widely reported, that the father Kashfi named on her marriage licence, Devi Kashfi, had died six weeks previously in India, only added to the intrigue. It was an inexplicable moment during a traumatic week for Kashfi – yet one that, twenty-two years later, she repeated in her autobiography, *Brando for Breakfast*:

According to Bosco [Devi Kashfi] had been 'fatally shot; the body was cremated a few hours later without an autopsy'.[34]

The day after Kashfi's 'honeymoon' statement to the press, her baptism certificate (babies born in India were routinely given baptism rather than birth certificates) was published in a British newspaper. William and Phoebe were both named as Joan O'Callaghan's parents; 'Brando's Bride Really is Welsh' said one headline, somewhat misleadingly.[35] Meanwhile, Howard Strickling claimed:

I didn't know her real name until this marriage business came up. We discovered by checking her passport and work permit that her name is O'Callaghan. Of course, we exploited the fact she was Indian. It's always a plus factor when an actress can be called an exotic import.[36]

Kashfi was indeed an 'exotic import' – even if her real name was O'Callaghan, and her erstwhile parents lived in Cardiff – whether she felt, at that particular moment, that it was a 'plus factor' is impossible to say.

Notes

[1] *Tri-City Herald*, 13 October 1957.

[2] *The New York Times,* 13 October 1957.

[3] Ibid.

[4] Darwin Porter, *Brando Unzipped*, (Blood Moon Productions, 2006), p. 518.

[5] Gary Carey, *Marlon Brando: The Only Contender*, (New English Library, 1986), p. 134.

[6] Stefan Kanfer, *Somebody: The Reckless Life and Remarkable Career of Marlon Brando*, (Faber and Faber, 2008), p. 158.

[7] Rene Jordan, *Marlon Brando*, (W.H. Allen, 1975), p. 80.

[8] Charles Higham, *Brando: The Unauthorized Biography*, (New American Library, 1987), p. 193.

[9] David Thompson, *Marlon Brando*, (DK Publishing, 2003), p. 94.

[10] Darwin Porter, *Brando Unzipped*, p. 526.

[11] Otto Friedrich, *City of Nets: A Portrait of Hollywood in the 1940s*, (Harper & Row, 1986), epigraph.

[12] E. J. Fleming, *The Fixers*, (McFarland & Company, 1954), p.2.

[13] Jeanine Basinger, *The Star Machine*, (Vintage Books, 2009), p. xiii.

[14] *Independent*, Long Beach, Calif. 14 October 1957.

[15] E. J. Fleming, *The Fixers*, p. 1.

[16] Jeanine Basinger, *The Star Machine*, p. 47.

[17] Otto Friedrich, *City of Nets: A Portrait of Hollywood in the 1940s*, pp. 354-355.

[18] *Parade*, 12 July 1959.

[19] Louella O. Parsons, 'Hollywood Scene', *The Stars and Stripes*, 24 December 1955.

[20] Louella O. Parsons, 'Louella's Movie-Go-Round', *Albuquerque Journal*, 4 June 1956.

[21] *Tri-City Herald*, 13 October 1957.

[22] *Oxnard Press-Courier*, 14 October 1957.

[23] *Chester Times* 14 October 1957.

[24] *The Independent* 14 October 1957.

[25] *South Wales Echo* 17 October 1957.

[26] Ibid.

[27] *The Florence Morning News*, 18 October 1957.

[28] *The Bridgeport Telegram* 18 October 1957.

[29] Charles Higham, *Brando: The Unauthorized Biography*, p. 193.

[30] *The New York Times*, 13 October 1957.

[31] Peter Manso, *Brando*, (Weidenfeld & Nicolson, 1994), p. 463.

[32] *The Salt Lake Tribune*, 18 October 1957.

[33] *The Cedar Rapids Gazette*, 14 October 1957.

[34] Anna Kashfi Brando & E.P. Stein, *Brando for Breakfast*, (Crown Publishers, 1979), p. 103.

[35] *Syracuse Herald Journal*, 15 October 1957.

[36] Ibid.

4

Who *Was* Brando's Bride?

'Some people say my daughter looks Indian, that she is dark-skinned. Well maybe she gets that from my mother. She was French and came from Dijon, in the south.'

William O'Callaghan
Chicago Daily Tribune, October 19th 1957

RAILWAY PEOPLE, RAILWAY LIVES...

Chakradharpur is a railway town – at least since the 1890s when the first seventy-two miles of track connecting it with the Bengal Nagpur Railway were laid. Located in Eastern India in the heart of the Chota Nagpur Plateau, it was a quiet place surrounded by mountains and lush green jungle with the Sanjay River running through its eastern fringes. It was a peaceful town of mixed cultures where all four of the major religions – Christianity, Islam, Sikhism and Hinduism – co-existed. In the 1920s it was home to supporters of Indian Independence, Gandhi, and the Khilifat Movement against the British. A decade later it was where William and Phoebe O'Callaghan were living when their daughter Joan was born.

The railways were an important source of both employment and status for Anglo-Indians. The British treated them as a 'buffer community'; they spoke English as well as the local language, they could get the job done and they helped seal the relationship between British and Indian workers. Mindful that the railways were a symbol of imperial power and therefore could be sabotaged, a space was created 'for the Anglo-Indians to keep the racial politics vis-à-vis Indians intact.'[1] The railways were not the only area where the British depended on the Anglo-Indians. According to Anglo-Indian historian Beverley Pearson, without their support British rule would have collapsed:

> We ran the railways, post and telegraph, police and customs, education, export and import, shipping, tea, coffee and tobacco plantations, the coal and gold fields... If it had any value the British made sure we ran it.[2]

Railway towns, like Chakradharpur tended to be divided into three distinct communities: the Railway Lines, the cantonments, and the city. The cantonments were where the British lived – originally military bases which during the 19th century were developed into fully fledged small towns of their own with parks, shops, churches and schools. According to John Masters in *Bhowani Junction*, his novel about an Anglo-Indian community in pre-Independence India, the city was where 'God knows how many thousand Indians are packed in like sardines'. Railway people, like the O'Callaghans, lived and worked in a part of town known as the 'Railway Lines' (also called 'Railway Colonies'), an area built to accommodate employees and their families. This was where a particular kind of British culture and social position predicated on notions of race, caste and hierarchy was preserved.

Indian railway mania had been under way since the 1840s when the then Governor-General of India, Lord Hardinge, allowed private entrepreneurs to launch a rail system. The clamour for an Indian railway network was fuelled, in part, by British businessmen who 'saw the new lines thrusting inland as levers opening up new markets and sources of raw materials' and came to fruition in the middle of the 19th century.[3] Two companies were created and, with assistance from the East India Company, railways were hastily constructed across India during the next half century. The technological advances epitomised progress and would be useful for everything from eliminating Hindu Nationalism to profiting British businessmen who were encouraged from the beginning to invest heavily with the promise of a good return on their money.

Railways were to transform the story of India – and to play a major role in the lives of both of Kashfi's parents.

William O'Callaghan would one day tell journalists that, 'both the missus and me were born in London',[4] and that Joan lived in India while he worked as a traffic superintendent with Indian Railways implying, strongly, that they were simply living there for his job. The truth is that both William and Phoebe were born into railway families who were already rooted in India. The two Henrys (Henry O'Callaghan, William's father, and Henry Shrieves, Phoebe's father) were engine drivers who worked for the Bengal Nagpur Railway (BNR). William himself was working as the station master in Chakradharpur when he met Phoebe.

In the Railway Lines each employee rented their home from the company. Accommodation was allocated according to their status – junior staff in a tenement or two storey flat, while middle management had spacious bungalows with servants' quarters at the back of the compound. Barrack-like living quarters were provided a little way off from the bungalows for the washer-men, sweepers, gardeners and cooks. There were tarmacked roads, stone slab pavements, hedges, shady trees and areas for children to play in. Social conduct was well defined and adhered to rigidly; a hierarchy was maintained at all times. The British and the Irish held the top jobs but the railways functioned through the mid-and lower-level jobs which were held by Anglo-Indians. Due to the ease with which the community got the jobs during the British era, Indians dubbed it their 'grandfather's property'.[5]

Children attended the Railway School unless, like the O'Callaghan children, they were sent away to boarding school. Religion played a central role in the community. Grace was said before every meal, whether you were Anglican or Catholic and church – to which the women wore their best clothes with scarves or straw hats – was attended twice on a Sunday. The dresses were specially tailored, according to designs from the English Fashion Book sent over from England, by Muslim tailors who worked on the verandas of the houses and were paid according to the number of dresses sewn on the day. But it was the Institute which was the heart and soul of each Railway Colony. Much like the traditional Working-Men's Clubs in Britain (except that the Institute was designed for families) there was a range of social activities – as Olive Lennon, a former teacher from a railway school recalled: there was 'never a dull moment; movies, card games and heavy-schedule social evenings.'[6]

For Anglo-Indians this way of life lasted for less than seventy years – from the birth of the railways until India gained her independence. Once the Anglo-Indian community no longer enjoyed the exclusive privileges afforded to them by the British many left India altogether. Those that stayed, and wanted to remain on the railways now competed alongside Indians for jobs which had always been theirs under British rule.

PHOEBE'S STORY

The story of the O'Callaghan family in India is fragmented by denial, doubt and the corrosive consequences of British Imperialism. Phoebe Shrieves, Kashfi's mother, is the key to most of this narrative. Her story represents one aspect of British rule in India from the eighteenth-century onwards.

She was born Martha Phoebe Melinda Shrieves in Chakradharpur in 1907, some one hundred and twenty years after her great-great-grandfather, John Shrieves the Elder, is believed to have arrived in India. Little is known about Shrieves the Elder other than that he was born in England and that, in 1783, he 'probably' boarded a ship named Francis and sailed to India. 'Probably' – because although a John Shreeves arrived in India in 1783 there is no record of the Francis sailing in 1783 –and when it sailed the following year there is no record of a John Shreeves being on board. What we *do* know for definite is that thirteen years later he was married and living in Trichinopoly, a district in the Presidency of Madras in British India. To put this in its historical context and understand *why* Shrieves the Elder found himself so far from home at the end of the 18th century it is necessary to know something about the British East India Company. The organisation, described by William Dalrymple as 'a powerful multinational corporation whose revenue-collecting operations were protected by its own private army', occupied and controlled vast swathes of the Indian continent between 1774 and 1858. They were a London trading company who were granted an exclusive charter to trade with India by Queen Elizabeth I. How a British company transformed themselves from traders to governors is a complex and bloody story of greed, opportunism, violence and chaos. This was the toxic foundation upon which the jewel in the crown of the British Empire was built. Following the first War of Independence in 1857, when Indian troops in the British army tried to overthrow the British Raj (described by one historian as an 'interlude' at which 'no Englishman of intellectual honesty can look without embarrassment and unhappiness.'),[7] the rule of the British East India Company was transferred to the British Crown (known as the British Raj – raj literally translates as rule in Hindi) and Queen Victoria was declared Empress of India.

According to military records, Shrieves was stationed at the garrison in Trichinopoly – he was a gunner in the 2nd Battalion Coast Artillery.[8] His wife was an Indian woman called Mariamab.[9] In the late eighteenth-century and early nineteenth-century it was fairly common for British officers and soldiers to marry local Indian women – in fact the East India Company had positively encouraged it, believing it might help to keep the peace between the newcomers and the established population. So keen were they, in fact, that they paid fifteen silver rupees for each child born to an Indian mother and a European father, as a family allowance. The children were amalgamated into the growing Anglo-Indian community – 'a deliberate act of self-preservation by the English.'[10]

Shrieves the Elder and Mariamab's first child, Benjamin was born in 1796 and lived for a year. Five years later, John and Mariamab's second child, John Shrieves the Younger, was born. Shrieves the Elder died in service on an unknown date. Of Mariamab there is no record of her place of birth, her father's name or the date of her death. Their surviving son, John Shrieves the Younger, does exist in records, letters and court documents and it is these primary sources which provide some details of what life was like for a mixed-race family in 19th century India.

At the age of eighteen Shrieves the Younger married Mary Goostree in Trichonopoly.[11] He was a clerk ('writer') by the time both he and Mary (who was illiterate) were orphans. Mary and Shrieves the Younger had four children: (John) Stephen, Marianne, Samuel and Benjamin. After Mary's early death, Shrieves the Younger followed his father into the military and became a Sergeant Major in the 31st Regiment of the Madras Native Regiment. While stationed in Bellary he became interested in missionary work. His second wife, Phoebe Coultrup, was the youngest daughter of Parker Coultrup (a missionary who was born in Kent) who had married an Anglo-Indian woman.[12] Phoebe and Shrieves the Younger married at Vepery in 1835. The following year he left the army and applied to the London Missionary Society for a position as an assistant missionary at Bellary.[13]

By that time the London Missionary Society (LMS) had been working in Bellary for a quarter of a century. It was founded in England in 1795 by evangelical Anglicans and Nonconformists to 'spread the knowledge of Christ among heathen and other unenlightened nations'.[14] Notable LMS missionaries include David Livingstone and the Olympic Gold Medallist Eric Liddell. Shrieves the Younger quickly impressed his new employers who noted he was a 'very diligent student and is making progress in the acquisition of the Teloogoo dialect creditable both to his talents & industry.'[15] (Telugu – next to Hindi and Bengali – is the third most spoken language in India).

Phoebe Coultrup Shrieves had seven children: Priscilla, Annie Sarah, John, Parker, Ebenezer, an unnamed girl and James. With the four children from Shrieves the Younger's first marriage, they were now a family of thirteen.[16] In his early fifties, Shrieves the Younger was struck down with paralysis and died a few months later leaving the family in dire financial straits. Less than a year later his son Benjamin, who had been supporting the family, died as did his two brothers, Stephen and Samuel, the following year. Phoebe lived to see the surviving children married before dying at the age of fifty-nine in 1871.[17]

Ebenezer Coultrup Shrieves, Phoebe O'Callaghan's grandfather and Kashfi's great-grandfather, was just fourteen when his father (Shrieves the Younger) died. Little is known about his life save that he was in 'Government service'. According to records he married Annie Dunning in Mysore in May 1866 and they had five boys: Ebenezer, Alfred, George, Charles and Henry. Henry Shrieves, the baby of the family, was born in 1882 – a century after his great-grandfather had arrived in India. Sixty years later he would leave the country of his birth and settle in Brighton.[18] His eldest daughter, Phoebe, with her husband William and their two children, Joan and Bosco, would follow him to England several months later.

As a young man Henry made his way from Bellary to Chakradharpur, in West Bengal, and began work as an engine driver for the Bengal-Nagpur Railway. He married a woman called Mary Melinda and, in May 1907, they had a daughter, Martha Phoebe Melinda Shrieves (Kashfi's mother), who was known as Phoebe. She was born in Chakradharpur and baptised the following day in nearby Chaibasa, a small town just west of the Raru River.[19] When Phoebe was three, her mother Mary died of pulmonary tuberculosis and was buried in the military cemetery at Fort William in Calcutta. Phoebe was placed in an orphanage where she remained, despite Henry remarrying four years later. The consequences of this early trauma may have reverberated down the years for Phoebe and her children. Years later Kashfi would say bitterly, 'she had a very difficult life, I have to say that because her mother died, you know, and she was put in an orphanage and all that kind of crap, and I guess that's what affected her.'[20] When Henry remarried he was thirty-two and his second wife, also called Phoebe and of Anglo-

Indian Portuguese decent, was fifteen – just eight years older than his daughter.

When she was twenty-four Phoebe Shrieves married William O'Callaghan.[21] She probably met him in the township established during the 'British era' and located on the eastern side of Chakradharpur – perhaps at a dance at the Railway Institute. William was, at the time, working for the Bengal Nagpur Railway as a Deputy Head Controller in Jamshedpur some forty miles from Chakradharpur.

WILLIAM'S STORY

William Patrick Michael O'Callaghan was twenty-eight when he married Phoebe Shrieves. According to his death certificate he was born in Calcutta in 1901 but beyond that fact his story is infuriatingly obscure – a strange brew of misinformation and mystery. There are many questions: why, for instance, is there no evidence of the existence of Peter O'Callaghan, William's grandfather, other than his name? His daughter Joan's school records in Darjeeling state that William was Irish and Phoebe Anglo-Indian yet he told journalists in the 1950s that his mother (who was born in India) was French and came from Dijon. And *why* did he say, while standing outside his home in Newfoundland Road in Cardiff in October 1957, words that he knew not to be true, words which turned his daughter into a liar in the eyes of the world: 'she has no Indian blood in her whatsoever'?[22] Why were different lives invented? The answer lies buried in how life was for some Anglo-Indians displaced from their home-land to somewhere they had always called home.

Like Phoebe, William was a motherless child. Henry O'Callaghan, William's father, married Agnes Boodrie in 1890 in Kamptee, a small town just outside Nagpur in the state of Maharashtra.[23] He was twenty-two and she was eighteen. Kamptee, originally known as Camp-T after its geographical shape, was founded when the British established a military cantonment there in 1821. It was a flourishing centre for trade even before the arrival of the railway in the late 19th century. Henry was an engine driver with the Bengal-Nagpur Railway. The only other fact known about him is that his father was called Peter O'Callaghan and of Peter there is nothing else in the records. Anna Kashfi said that her 'father's father was Irish' – and, given that an estimated 20% of the British population in India was Irish in 1817 and that the archetypal Irishman on the sub-continent was neither a missionary or a merchant, a doctor or an administrator but a soldier, it is possible to speculate that Peter O'Callaghan was recruited from Ireland before or after the Indian Uprising in 1857.[24] If that was the case – he was in for the long haul. If you enlisted in the British Army between 1847 and 1870 you served twenty-one years so it seems unlikely that he would have made it back to Ireland. Even less is known about Henry O'Callaghan's mother – there are no surviving records to tell us whether she was Irish, Indian or English, or whether she had any other children. However, given that his descendants grew up in the Anglo-Indian community, it is likely that she was either Indian or of Indian descent.

Agnes Boodrie, William's mother, is easier to trace through existing records. Her parents, Joseph and Ellen Boodrie, were married in Agra in 1858 and had four children, Walter, Minnie, Agnes and Alice – all of whom were probably born in Indore (known as 'mini- Bombay' because it had nearly as many cotton mills) where Joseph worked for the newly established British Raj in the Telegraph department.

The first of Henry and Agnes's three children, Evellina, was born in 1894 in Dongargarh, a small town about one hundred and twenty-five miles from Nagpur where the family were living. Six years later Terence arrived followed by William in 1901. Agnes died of a fever when William was three months old as did seven-year-old Terence within the year. Henry, aged thirty-eight and by now a Locomotive Foreman with the Bengal Nagpur Railway, married seventeen-year-old Nora Gladys McConochie when William was four. Henry and Nora's daughter, Gladys Amelia Margaret O'Callaghan, arrived in 1906 and was baptised in the Catholic Church of Our Lady of the Happy Voyage in Howrah (probably the same church in which Joan O'Callaghan's other grandfather, Henry Shrieves, married his second wife Phoebe D'Cunnah some eight years later).

William and Phoebe's first child, Joan Mary O'Callaghan, was born in the Eden Hospital in Calcutta in September 1934 and baptised a week later in Chakradharpur.[25] By the time Joan's brother, Bosco, arrived two years later, the O'Callaghan family had moved to Adra, an important railway town with a population which was 90% Anglo-Indian. William had been promoted to 'Head Train Controller', a senior position on the railways which entitled his family to travel in their own private railway carriage complete with their own chef. The family of four would remain in India for another twelve years. In 1948, one hundred and sixty-five years after John Shrieves the Elder had left Britain, his descendants returned to the place they had always called home.

There was, undoubtedly, 'Indian blood' in both William and Phoebe, although they either didn't know it, or chose not to recognise it. Their daughter, however, did:

> Well, I would say you would call me an Anglo-Indian because I have a lot of Indian blood in me. But way, way back [from] somebody, I don't know the story, but why would I come out like this?[26]

Somewhere in the nine years between leaving India in August 1948 and finding themselves unexpectedly cross-examined about their background in October 1957, the family altered their story of themselves. Joan O'Callaghan altered it again, and then again.

Notes

[1] *Hindustan Times*, 5 July 2015.

[2] Beverley Pearson 'Three Hundred Years in Ten Minutes (A Very Brief History of the Anglo-Indians)', October 2005 http://www.margaretdeefholts.com/angloindianhistory.html

[3] Lawrence James, *Raj: The Making of British India*, (Little, Brown and Company, 2003), p. 185.

[4] *The Daily Review*, 12 October 1957.

[5] *Hindustan Times,* 5 July 2015.

[6] Ibid.

[7] Philip Mason, *The Men Who Ruled India*, (Rupa & Co, 1985), p. 154.

[8] The British Library: Madras Muster Rolls and Casualty Returns (L/MIL/11/120) – 'Register of the Honorable Company's Effective European Troops on the Coast of Coromandel as they stood on 31st December 1800 (first section, no.2143)'.

[9] The British Library: Asia, Pacific and Africa Collections: Burial entry for son, Benjamin Shrieves, N/2/o/5/75.

[10] Beverley Pearson 'Three Hundred Years in Ten Minutes', http://www.margaretdeefholts.com/angloindianhistory.html

[11] The British Library: Asia, Pacific and Africa Collections: marriage entry N/2/7/455.

[12] The British Library: Asia, Pacific and Africa Collections: marriage entry N/2/17/36.

[13] James Sibree, *London Missionary Society: A Register of Missionaries, Deputations etcs, 1796-1923* (London, LMS, 1923).

[14] London Missionary Society at SOAS, University of London, http://www.mundus.ac.uk/cats/4/251.htm

[15] Letter from John Reid at Bellary 12 June 1836 to the Reverend William Ellis, Foreign Secretary to the LMS, SOAS.

[16] Letter from Phoebe Shrieves to LMS Board 17 November 1856: Annual Schedules of Returns of Bellary Mission to LMS (LMS records in SOAS).

[17] The British Library: Asia, Pacific and Africa Collections: burial entry N/2/52/190.

[18] Ancestry United Kingdom Incoming passenger lists. Ref TNA/BT26/.

[19] The British Library: Asia, Pacific and Africa Collections: baptism entry N/1/344/26.

[20] Sarah Broughton, 'Unpublished Recorded Interviews with Anna Kashfi', April 2009.

[21] The British Library: Asia, Pacific and Africa Collections: marriage entry N/1/537/81.

[22] *Los Angeles Examiner,* 15 October 1957.

[23] The British Library: Asia, Pacific and Africa Collections: marriage entry N/1/213/255.

[24] Sarah Broughton, 'Unpublished Recorded Interviews with Anna Kashfi', April 2009.

[25] Baptism Certificate information: St. Xavier's Church, Calcutta, 1934.

[26] Sarah Broughton, 'Unpublished Recorded Interviews with Anna Kashfi', April 2009.

5

Cardiff

1948 – 1953

My mother and stepfather had taken up residence in Ogmore-by-Sea, a small resort town on the coast of Wales.

Anna Kashfi, *Brando for Breakfast*

Things known to be true: **One** – Joan Mary O'Callaghan was born in Calcutta on September 30th 1934. **Two** – in late 1948 or early 1949 Joan O'Callaghan and her family left the small resort town of Ogmore-by-Sea on the coast of Wales and headed twenty miles up the road to Cardiff. **Three** – nine years later Joan, now known to the world as Anna Kashfi, the 'Grace Kelly of India', married Marlon Brando, the world's biggest film star.[1] Somewhere between those dates is the Cardiff where Joan spent her teenage years, the Cardiff that was staggering and swaggering unsteadily back onto its feet after the war. Anna Kashfi has never really acknowledged the five or so years she lived in the city yet Cardiff hangs around this story like a fading bruise: when you press the place it once was, only the memory of it still hurts – but it's there.

Cardiff in 1948: a forty-three-year-old city with twenty-four cinemas – including the Gaiety, the Gala and the

Globe, the Park Hall, the Plaza and the Prince of Wales – and a pub on every corner. The Rialto Cinema in Whitchurch was Joan O'Callaghan's local 'bughouse' where at Christmas each child was given an orange, courtesy of the management.[2] Cinemas in 1948 were places where, 'that ribbon of dreams as Orson Welles so eloquently described it, [took] us to somewhere we have not been to before but to where we keep returning'.[3] All the big Hollywood stars came to the city: Cary Grant, Montgomery Clift and Laurel and Hardy. Even the future president, Ronald Reagan, turned up in 1948 to promote his latest movie, *The Voice of the Turtle* – shortly after warning the House Committee on Un-American Activities of the dangers of a witch-hunt in Hollywood.

Cardiff in 1948 was the Maskrey's, Marments and Mackross shops. It was afternoon tea in the Angel or the Royal Hotel and dances at the Regal or Bindles or St Cyprian's Hall. But these were the lighter moments. Abortion, suicide and gay relationships were still illegal. Capital punishment was legal. Mahmoud Mattan, a Somali-born sailor, was the last person to be hanged in Cardiff. At his trial in 1952, he was described by his own barrister as a 'semi-civilised savage'.[4] It was Cardiff seamen who established the largest British-born Somali population in the country.[5] Mattan was part of the generations of young men who were originally drawn to the city to work in the thriving docks after the opening of the Suez Canal. These young men arrived as sailors at the end of the 19th century, not as refugees or slaves, driven by the desire to earn money to buy more livestock in Somalia. Because of Britain's colonial presence in Somalia it was possible for Somalis to live and work in the United Kingdom – and there was plenty of work available, for the seamen in the docks anyway, and later in the steel industry. Often though, they were filling jobs that white workers didn't want – whether on the tramp steamers where the working conditions were tough, or in the merchant navy during the First World War when the white British seamen were transferred into the Royal Navy. Some of them settled down with local women – like Mattan. In 1945 when he was twenty-two he met and married seventeen-year-old Laura Williams from the Rhondda Valley. Such was the level of racism against him that the couple and their three sons were vilified by their neighbours and forced to live apart, in separate houses, on the same street.[6] Mahmoud Mattan had worked as a steelworker until he was made redundant. In March of 1952 he was accused of murdering a shopkeeper named Lily Volpert on Bute Street in the Butetown area of Cardiff Docks. His defence was that he was at the cinema and then at home but key evidence from an eyewitness called Harold Cover claimed that he had seen Mattan coming out of Lily Volpert's shop at the time of the murder. He was found guilty and hanged in Cardiff prison on the 3rd September 1952. Nearly fifty years later, after decades of campaigning by Mattan's widow Laura and her family, Michael Mansfield, Britain's most high-profile defence lawyer, fought to have the conviction quashed. He established that Cover had not mentioned in court, as he had in his eyewitness statement, that the Somali man he described leaving the shop had a gold tooth (which Mattan did not have). It also emerged that the police had traced a Somali man named Taher Gass who lived on Bute Street, had a gold tooth and had also admitted passing the shop three times on the night of the murder. Gass was convicted of a different murder two years later and committed to Broadmoor. Cover had received a reward of £200 – which in 1952 would have bought him a house in Cardiff. Although Mansfield's forensic review of the case cleared Mattan's name in the Court of Appeal in 1998, making him the first person to have their conviction quashed in Britain after being executed, the twenty-nine-year-old immigrant had paid for the flawed handling of his case with his life.

The first Indian woman student in Cardiff arrived in 1947. Pushpa Kapila studied English, Economics and History and was the first woman from South Asia to graduate from Cardiff University. She returned to India and embarked upon a career as a pioneering lawyer. She wore white saris. After her death in 2013 her son, Aman Hingorani, recalled that it 'made people exclaim and wonder if she was "a priestess or a princess"'.[7] Cardiff was all heavy shoes, suits and hats, cloth caps and mufflers – no wonder an Indian girl in a sari was a sight to behold. Yet this was the same Cardiff that was rumoured to have more than fifty different nationalities living and working side by side in Butetown.[8] It was the same Cardiff where Mahmoud Mattan had met his Laura. Journalist Albert Lloyd, writing in the *Picture Post* in the early 1950s, described Butetown as 'the nearest thing we have to a ghetto in this free land, with its inhabitants marked off from the rest of the city not only by social barriers and the old Great Western Railway Bridge but also by race prejudice.' He quoted a Somali seaman: 'If I go up into town, say to the pictures, why man, everybody looks at me as if I left some buttons undone.' Despite this, one of the first studies of the attitudes of whites towards the immigrant community, published in 1948 and based on fieldwork carried out in Butetown, was hopeful about the 'latent friendliness' that lay beneath the surface appearance of apathy and even overt prejudice – although Lloyd also conceded that 'relatively few English people have made close contact with coloured people.'[9]

The Second World War had left its mark upon Cardiff in different ways. After the fall of France, the city was within easy flying range for the Luftwaffe and, on January 2nd 1941, the blitz began. Llandaff Cathedral was shattered, but worse horrors were reserved for the districts of Canton, Grangetown and Riverside where more than one hundred and fifty people were killed. Six days later most were buried in a mass grave. The final air raid on the city took place on May 18th 1943. The press claimed that it was in retaliation for the Dambusters' raid which had been carried out the day before.[10] The Dambusters' raid was famously led by Wing Commander Guy Gibson. Less well known is the fact that Wing Commander Gibson spent time in Cardiff after marrying the actress Eve Turner in Penarth where Turner was born. Penarth, along with Cardiff, became a 'port of entry' for troops and equipment from the United States during the war.[11]

After the boom years of the war, when Cardiff resembled an arsenal as factories in and around the city produced cartridges, shells, parachutes and guns, there was the problem of how to retain or replace its manufacturing industries. The docks continued the decline which had begun a quarter of a century earlier and the flow of military traffic ceased as the ships returned to their home ports. More significantly, coal exports were barely reaching a million tonnes. In the Llanishen district of the city, the Royal Ordinance factory continued to produce weapons and, in 1948, employed over a thousand people. Engineering firms such as John Curran and John Williams also provided a foundation for heavy industry. Curran's Metals and Munitions Limited was a famously Catholic firm founded in 1914 by Edward Curran, based on the Taff Embankment, and this was where William O'Callaghan began work when he arrived in Cardiff in the late 1940s.[12] It was also where, in 1952, fourteen-year-old Shirley Bassey followed her sisters into the factory. By the time she arrived, Curran's speciality was making baths and enamelware. Shirley worked in the packing shed, an all-female department with a male supervisor, for three pounds a week. She later described the work to the chat show host Russell Harty as 'wrapping pee pots in brown paper'.[13] The rest of the firm was very much a man's world. William O'Callaghan was always referred to as a 'factory worker' in the newspaper reports. He himself told an American reporter, Doug Brewer, who door-stepped him in 1957, 'I'm just a poor man. I work in a factory near here. I earn a few pounds a week. Is my daughter ashamed of me for this?'[14] The disparity between O'Callaghan's former status and circumstances in India and his job in his adopted city must have been significant and surely would have required a major adjustment.

For the children of William O'Callaghan, his fourteen-

year-old daughter, Joan, and twelve-year-old son, Bosco,
life in Cardiff must also have taken some getting used to.
They had settled in the (white) Gabalfa district, on the
outskirts of the city centre on Newfoundland Road which
was sandwiched between the main arteries of North Road
and Whitchurch Road; one of a group of roads near St
Joseph's Church known as 'the Colonies' (they were named
after outposts of the British Empire). Newfoundland Road
was also the birthplace of the poet R. S. Thomas; he lived
at No. 5 between 1913 and 1918. Thirty years later, the
O'Callaghan's began renting No. 100, a three bedroomed,
bay-fronted 'semi' described by Doug Brewer as 'two-
storied, neat, poor, proud' in his article for *Modern
Screen*.[15] It was within walking distance of Cardiff
University where Indian student Pushpa Kapila was study-
ing. More importantly, for the O'Callaghans, there was a
close-knit Catholic community on the doorstep. William
and Phoebe were devout, attending Mass at 8am each
morning at St Joseph's Church on nearby New Zealand
Road.[16] Joan was sent to St Joseph's Convent School, a
Catholic school, on North Road. She made an impression,
even at that early age: the Sister-in-charge reported that,
'She was a well-behaved girl and good at her schoolwork.
She was very dignified, I remember, and even in those
days very striking in appearance.'[17] Joan's previous school
had been St Helen's Convent in Kurseong, Darjeeling.

After Joan left school she worked as a cashier in Joe
Dale's butcher's shop for six months, in a café in
Porthcawl, a seaside town twenty-five miles from Cardiff
famous for its Coney Beach Pleasure Park, and spent a
year at Cardiff College of Art. It was the butcher's shop

and the art college that the journalists descended upon, as well as St Joseph's Convent School. Joe Dale, 'the jovial butcher', said:

> She was a good girl at her job, handling our money. She worked here six months. She was a beauty and I knew she wouldn't stay long. Boys stopped to look thru [sic] the window at her. She wanted to be an artist. Good luck to her I say.[18]

Beauty was a recurring theme; June Tiley, one of Joan O'Callaghan's teachers said, 'I think she was one of the most naturally beautiful girls I've ever seen.' And a class-mate of Joan's at the art college, Eliza Maddalena, echoed this:

> She was so quiet that if she hadn't been pretty, she would never have stood out in a crowd. What exquisite colouring! Lots of Irish have that colouring, but I would have taken her for Spanish. I'd never have said that she was Indian.[19]

Margaret Phelps, a school-friend from St Joseph's Convent:

> She was a real ugly duckling, afraid of boys, that was until she got to be sixteen. Then she became very pretty and the boys all ran after her.[20]

And even after Joan left Cardiff for post-war, rubble strewn London, Henry Noble, the owner of the fur shop Noble Furs of Regent Street, said he had hired Joan just to stand in his store and look beautiful:

> I paid her six guineas a week. But I couldn't keep her. She
> left me to work in an Indian fashion shop, modelling saris.
> The next thing we knew she was off to Hollywood.[21]

The Indian fashion shop, in Piccadilly Circus, called The
Maharajah was owned by a woman called Selma Ghose.
This was the name Anna Kashfi gave as her mother's
when she married Marlon Brando. The rest of her life in
London, from the age of around eighteen until she left
Britain for America on her twenty-first birthday, is hard
to piece together – but the odd fragment survives. At one
stage she shared a flat with Belinda Lee, a drama student
who became a Rank starlet in 1954. After Kashfi married
Brando, Lee defended her former flatmate:

> To me Anna is as Indian as the beautiful saris she loves
> to wear. I am astonished everyone disputes it. And I
> should know, for we shared a flat together for months
> when I was a R.A.D.A student and she was a model. We
> were usually broke and I cannot think of anyone better
> as a room-mate under those circumstances. Our doorbell
> was always ringing. We never had any shortage of dates
> but most visitors were for Anna. Whenever we had a good
> natter together, Anna always talked about India. She told
> me her parents were Indian and that she was born in
> Calcutta. I am happy to go on record as saying Anna
> Kashfi really is an Indian girl. Just as she says she is.[22]

Lee and Kashfi both suffered the fate of being dismissed

as notorious women, not only that – a scandal in Lee's private life was to virtually destroy her career, just as *this* scandal destroys Kashfi's.

Various contradictory accounts – Kashfi, her father and others – all tell how Kashfi leapt from shop girl to model to a role in *The Mountain*. However it happened, Joan O'Callaghan did go to Paris, was cast in the film, and did leave London, Cardiff and Ogmore-by-Sea behind her in pursuit of an American dream.

Notes

[1] Louella O. Parsons, 'Hollywood Scene', *The Stars and Stripes*, 24 December 1955.

[2] Gary Wharton, *Ribbon of Dreams: Remembering the Cardiff Cinemas*, Mercia Cinema Society, 1998, p. 95.

[3] Ibid., p. vi.

[4] Stephen Khan, 'Tormented Life and Death of Man in Black', *The Guardian* 3 August 2003.

[5] 'Somalis in Cardiff', *The Guardian*, 23 January 2006.

[6] Jason Bennetto, 'Racial hatred led to a legalised lynching', *The Independent*, 25 February 1998.

[7] *Indian Express*, 2 February 2014.

[8] Glenn Jordan, *'Down the Bay': Picture Post, Humanist Photography and Images of 1950s Cardiff*, Butetown History & Arts Centre, 2001, p. 10.

[9] *Picture Post*, 22 April 1950.

[10] Major Hugo Jones obituary, *The Telegraph*, 11 February 2011.

[11] Dennis Morgan, *The Cardiff Story*, Hackman Printers, 2001, p. 231.

[12] John L. Williams, *Miss Shirley Bassey*, Quercus, 2010, p. 53.

[13] Ibid.

[14] Doug Brewer, 'The Truth about Marlon's Wife', *Modern Screen*, December 1957.

[15] Ibid.

[16] Sarah Broughton, 'Unpublished Recorded Interview with Sister Thomasina O'Driscoll', September 2008.

[17] *Empire News and Sunday Chronicle*, 20 October 1957.

[18] *Chicago Daily Tribune*, 19 October 1957.

[19] Doug Brewer, 'The Truth about Marlon's Wife', *Modern Screen*, December 1957.

[20] *Chicago Daily Tribune*, 19 October 1957.

[21] Ibid.

[22] *Empire News and Sunday Chronicle*, 20 October 1957.

6

Constructing Anna

'She's the one. Pack the bags. We're rolling.'[1]

Spencer Tracy, after meeting Anna Kashfi in 1955

Knowing how much their business depended on movie stars, and knowing how much young actors and actresses (or waitresses and gas jockeys) wanted to become movie stars, the studios created a plan to locate suitable candidates, hire them, fix 'em up, and put 'em on the market.[2]

Jeanine Basinger, *The Star Machine*

A four line item in Frank Morriss's HERE THERE *and* HOLLYWOOD column announced the arrival of 'Anna Kashfi' to American film fans in September 1955:

> Anna Kashfi, exotic 19-year-old actress from India by way of London and Paris, will have the top feminine lead opposite Tracy... She'll portray the Hindu woman found in the wreckage of a plane high in the Alps and brought to the valley below in a suspense-laden trek led by Tracy...

Exotic is the first word used to describe Anna Kashfi and it's the one that sticks. For nearly two years she will be defined by this fact – until her right to be called exotic is called into question. As she will find out, being labelled Welsh or Irish does not entitle you to call yourself exotic. Her exotic appearance means that, during her brief career, she will be employed to play a Hindu, a Korean, a Mexican and, as the wife of African-American singer Nat King Cole, an unspecified 'exotic'. But for now, at the beginning of her life as Anna Kashfi, Joan O'Callaghan submitted herself to being 'created, carefully and cold-bloodedly, built up from nothing, from nobody... Age, beauty, talent – least of all talent – has nothing to do with it...'[3] Marlon Brando referred to this process as 'a lot of frozen monkey vomit' – his wife-to-be embraced it.[4]

There are a couple of different accounts of how Kashfi ended up in a hotel room with Spencer Tracy and Edward Dmytryk. Glynne Mortimer, a friend who was working for a theatrical agency, told her that Paramount Pictures were looking for an Indian-looking girl to play a non-speaking Hindu woman in a new film. William O'Callaghan says he was with Kashfi in London when they met a film producer, Richard Mealand, who invited her to play an Indian girl in a new film called *The Mountain* (Mealand had recently discovered a young Belgian woman named Audrey Hepburn playing a small role in a British film and had suggested her for *Roman Holiday* which began filming in the summer of 1952). Kashfi's account, published in her autobiography twenty-five years later, differed slightly; William is not present. Kashfi reported Mealand as saying:

Look, Paramount is doing a picture in France that calls for an Indian girl. The star has casting approval, and he is very difficult. We've interviewed seventeen girls so far, and they have all been turned down. The part requires you to speak only Hindi – no English. And the acting is only to react against the star. If you're interested, I can arrange an interview in Paris.[5]

Edward Dmytryk, in his autobiography, *It's a Hell of a Life But Not a Bad Living*, published two decades after Kashfi married Brando, recalled what happened next:

In Paris, Tracy and I spent an easy few days interviewing Indian actresses and eating in fine restaurants. There were plenty of the latter but very few of the former. I think we saw only four or five young women, and only one of these was suitable. Her name was Anna Kashfi, she came from London, and she looked lovely in a sari. The passport she carried bore an Irish name, but that made little difference to us. She looked Indian and she got the part. As an added inducement, my assistant, A. C. Lyles, promised to introduce her to Marlon Brando when we got back to Hollywood.[6]

Kashfi herself took a pragmatic view of her lucky break:

I think he wanted me because the part calls for Spencer Tracy to carry a girl up and down the mountain –and I was *so* skinny.[7]

Throughout the 1930s, 1940s and 1950s, film studios spent a small fortune on talent scouts who travelled around America and much of Europe looking for young men and women who could be turned into film stars.

Richard Mealand was one such scout and Joan O'Callaghan was young, beautiful and possibly talented. Most important of all, she was (apparently) obedient. Obedience was compulsory. For a machine to work, its components had to be under control. Jeanine Basinger provides a chilling foretaste of what lay in store for Kashfi when she ended up becoming what the studio feared most:

> With the amount of money it would take to promote, publicise, and turn out a movie star, studios didn't want any nasty surprises down the road. 'Nasty surprises' were not what people today might think. Crazy mothers and fathers who had disappeared? No problem. Shady reputations, unusual sexual practices, even alcoholism? Relatives in prison? The studios could – and did – handle all those. They knew how to shut up and cover up. Nobody cared about bad behaviour as long as it didn't make the newspapers. What they did care about was money. 'Nasty surprises' meant that initial investments weren't going to pay off. Maybe the star was going to be lazy, sickly, neurotic, or worst of all, disobedient and ungrateful. Anything that threatened the financial investment needed to be rooted out before it could become a nasty surprise.[8]

The Mountain began filming in the French Alps towards the end of August 1955. Publicity shots taken during filming, and published in the press the following month, picture Kashfi for the first time during what must have been an extraordinary period for her. Within eight short weeks her life had transformed utterly, and unexpectedly, from selling scarves in Piccadilly Circus to playing opposite Spencer Tracy and Robert Wagner, and her name had been changed to Anna Kashfi.

Being seen by a director who had then immediately cast her meant that Kashfi bypassed two key stages in the process of developing a potential star: the screen test and what was labelled 'a thorough physical analysis'. Any problems discovered in the course of this unsettling examination could be sorted out in 'fix-'em up time'.[9] Two years before Kashfi arrived in Los Angeles, the Judy Garland remake of *A Star is Born* fictionalised the practice in a memorable sequence where 'Esther Blodgett' is transformed into 'Vicki Lester'. In real life Hollywood, the whole lot was up for grabs – teeth, ears, noses, eyebrows, hairlines – and that was just appearances. Anything and everything could be transformed – from dodgy accents and stutters to troublesome mothers. Kashfi escaped all this largely unscathed – perhaps because the general feeling about her was overwhelmingly positive. Dorothy Manners, an American syndicated gossip columnist, is typical in this assessment of her:

We've never had anyone quite like her in pictures. Her skin is like beige ivory. She has limpid enormous brown eyes. Her mouth is made up American fashion with the fully curved underlip. Although she arrived with a trunk full of her native saris she dresses in slacks or simple cocktail dresses off the set. Anna is a fascinating blend of the old world and the new.[10]

Kashfi had found her niche.

After the change of name, the next key stage in the construction of a star was the 'fabricated biography', also known as a 'studio biography'.[11] These were essential because they defined the story that was going to be fed to the public – primarily where he or she came from and who the family was. They were, of course, designed to show the star in the best possible light with minor achievements magnified and anything uninteresting or unpleasant from the past either eliminated or altered beyond recognition. As Basinger notes:

> Fathers who were plumbers became engineers or architects; two years in a reform school could be recast as 'continuing his education'.[12]

Mickey Rooney agreed that studio biography bore little resemblance to reality:

> Instead of collecting blondes and redheads, they had me collecting stamps coins and matchboxes. My favourite author, according to this studio fantasy, was Eugene O'Neill. That would have implied that I read books. But I didn't read books. I barely read the plays I starred in.[13]

Kashfi's studio biographies recast her father's occupation *and* his name; William O'Callaghan, Head Train Controller, became Devi Kashfi, Architect or, sometimes, Civil Engineer. This paved the way for an exciting backdrop for Kashfi's entry to Hollywood involving a vaguely international lifestyle encompassing travel opportunities and several languages. Her world was being re-imagined as an exciting and appealing story and marketed as such.

The starting point for the 'studio bio' was a question-naire which covered everything from school, to favourite colour to best pet, even phobias – anything that the pub-licity department might be able to make use of. In Kashfi's case, as well as her language skills which apparently in-cluded 'fluent French, English, Hindu, three Indian dialects, some Italian, Spanish and German', her interests were transposed into the following information which was designed to endear her to American movie fans:

> She never cooked until she came to Hollywood but is having a ball with American recipes... loves tennis and skiing, but can't swim a stroke... crazy about American jazz ('especially boojeez-woojeez')... learning the Charleston... an avid reader, particularly of political commentaries on the Eastern Hemisphere... looks like something out of Vogue in American high fashions, but is explosive as an H-bomb in a native sari... keeps her private life private... loves to model in clay, paint, sketch and redecorate... and she's proud as punch about learning to drive since coming to Hollywood.[14]

Along with the 'studio bio' were the photographs. Every potential star, male or female, was brought into the pub-licity department and asked to pose for a range of shots from glamour, to girl or boy next door, to 'holiday' (stars dressed variously as Easter bunnies, pumpkins, Santas or Cupids). The publicity departments then released these to newspapers and magazines on a regular basis. They were space fillers – and free! Kashfi managed to avoid both the kitsch and the cheesecake poses on religious grounds (inappropriate for a Hindu girl) but did pose for both an Indian look (long, flowing hair and looking moodily at the camera while swathed in a sari) and All-American-style in pedal-pushers, hair tied back and a big smile.

Finally, after the studio bios and the photographs came the 'plants'. 'Plants' were the gradual drip-feeding of a new personality into the gossip columns which, if successful, would eventually be rewarded with an invitation to tea with Louella 'Lolly' Parsons or Hedda Hopper. Lolly and Hedda were notorious, they were, undoubtedly, the most terrifying women in Hollywood. Otto Friedrich is succinct in his damnation of the pair: 'It is almost impossible now to realize the power once exercised by Mrs Parsons, and her rival, Hedda Hopper, but in the 1940s, these two vain and ignorant women tyrannized Hollywood.'[15] In the 1950s, although their power was waning slowly, they were still crucial to a star arriving – and surviving.

Kashi's first substantial 'plant' was published on November 4th 1955. She was twenty-one years old, had been in Los Angeles for little more than a month — and the Studio knew that she was already involved with Marlon Brando (Harry Mines, Paramount's publicist, had given Brando Kashfi's phone number). The story which was syndicated in newspapers across the United States was: *Indian Girl, Anna Kashfi, is Champion of Male Sex.* Her fledgling persona was established; Kashfi was both an 'Indian beauty' and 'a living doll in any language' and her message was designed to play well across the conservative America of the 1950s:

> Exotic, pale-skinned Anna said the number one lesson in her upbringing was that the man should be made happy at all times. 'And I have been taught to believe,' she said, 'that a man is happiest when he is gazing at an attractive woman'.

Kashfi was to be perceived as acquiescent, yet wise:

> As for the art of conversation, Anna advocates listening before showing your ignorance.

Flirtatious:

> I never discuss myself because a man prefers to think he knows all about the woman he's with.

Yet moral:

> Even though I have been out in the world making a career as an actress and away from the strict beliefs and upbringing of my people, I still faithfully cling to the lesson I learned about the opposite sex.[16]

She is exotic enough to be interesting and Americanised enough to integrate – qualities which would serve her well over the next two years.

It is apparent, looking back, that the construction of Anna Kashfi owed much to her relationship with Marlon

Brando. Despite the fact that she is never openly acknowledged as his girlfriend (although there are numerous
'plants' about their dates during their two-year courtship)
Brando is ever present. Her fate feels inextricably, lethally,
linked with his from the very beginning.

Notes

[1] Anna Kashfi & E.P. Stein, *Brando for Breakfast*, (Crown Publishers, 1979), p. 18.

[2] Jeanine Basinger, *The Star Machine*, (Vintage Books, 2009), p. 19.

[3] Ibid., p. 11.

[4] Ibid., p. 3.

[5] Anna Kashfi, *Brando for Breakfast*, p. 18.

[6] Edward, Dmytryk, *It's a Hell of a Life But Not a Bad Living*, (Times Books, 1978), p. 202.

[7] Hedda Hopper, 'India to Hollywood', (syndicated column), 9 May 1956.

[8] Jeanine Basinger, *The Star Machine*, pp. 37-38.

[9] Ibid., p. 38, p. 40.

[10] Dorothy Manners, 'Anna Kashfi Blends Old World with New', (syndicated column), 9 February 1956.

[11] Mark Borkowski, *The Fame Formula*, (Sidgwick & Jackson, 2008), p. 183.

[12] Jeanine Basinger, *The Star Machine*, pp. 49-50.

[13] Mark Borkowski, *The Fame Formula*, pp. 183-184.

[14] MGM biographical information, Academy of Motion Picture, Arts And Sciences, Hollywood, 30 July 1956.

[15] Otto Friedrich, *City of Nets: A Portrait of Hollywood in the 1940s*, (Harper & Row, 1986), p. 92.

[16] *Kingsport News,* 4 November 1955.

7

Lightning Hits...

Cardiff Recalls Brando's Wife
Its Girls Sigh and Hope Lightning Hits Again

Surrounded by sausages, a pretty dark-haired girl sits in Dale's butcher shop here daydreaming. 'I'd like to marry Rock Hudson,' she said. 'Do you think I have many chances?' Over her head are two signs. One says 'Sausages, 1/6 a half pound.' The other says, 'Marlon Brando's wife worked here.'
Chicago Daily Tribune, October 19th 1957

In the autumn of 1955, while Britain was preoccupied with the thwarted romance between Princess Margaret and Group Captain Peter Townsend, the first rumour of a relationship between Marlon Brando and Anna Kashfi appeared in the American press:

HERE THERE and HOLLYWOOD with Frank Morriss
... Marlon Brando has been dating Anna Kashfi, the Indian beauty who is in Hollywood for a role opposite Spencer Tracy and Robert Wagner in *The Mountain*...[1]

Brando and Kashfi had met, like many couples, at work and in that most domestic of settings, the cafeteria (known in Hollywood as the commissary). Work for both of them at the time was at Paramount Pictures on Melrose Avenue in Hollywood – Kashfi because she was signed as a contract player and Brando because his production company, Pennebaker Productions, rented an office in the Paramount Studios grounds. Commissaries date back to the earliest days of the silent film era; they originated as places to feed studio employees swiftly and cheaply and quickly became the place to see and be seen. George Englund, Brando's business partner in Pennebaker Productions, recalled:

> If your offices were at Paramount there were three main places to have lunch – Oblath's coffee shop across the street, Lucy's on Melrose, and the studio commissary. We usually chose the commissary, it was animated, all the filmmaking principals were there.[2]

At Paramount, the commissary head was the legendary Pauline Kessinger; rumour had it that Adolph Zukor, who transformed Paramount Pictures into a major studio, found Mrs Kessinger standing on the lot in 1928 and built a commissary around her.[3]

Kessinger presided over an elegant dining room where the young stars sat at the so-called 'Golden Circle',[4] a large round table in the middle of the room covered in a gold cloth, which could be easily seen by producers and directors. The rest of the room was crowded with wooden cafeteria tables of varying heights. Established stars at Paramount, who in the 1950s included Charlton Heston, Audrey Hepburn, Grace Kelly and James Stewart as well as the phenomenally popular comedy duo Dean Martin and Jerry Lewis, knew they had arrived when a dish was named after them; Lamour Salad, Turkey and Eggs a la Crosby and Pie a la Lake were amongst the creations which honoured the studio's big hitters.

On the day in question Pauline Kessinger was, as always, on hand to greet guests and regulars as they walked through the dining room door. Marlon Brando was having lunch with Eva Marie Saint, his co-star from *On the Waterfront,* who was filming *That Certain Feeling*, a romantic comedy with Bob Hope. According to Kashfi, 'It was there, while nibbling at her nape that his eyes turned to a nearby table, and he mumbled, "Who is that good-looking broad in the red sari?"'[5]

Startlingly beautiful and dressed in a dark red sari (Hindu brides always wear red saris because they symbolise fertility) with gold trimming, Kashfi would have expected to turn heads – but this was the Paramount commissary and *The Ten Commandments* (one of Paramount's biggest box office hits) and *War and Peace* were just two of the films in production at the time. Consequently the room was packed with Hebrew slaves and 19th century Russians and a 'good-looking broad in a red sari' was perhaps not so extraordinary. Then again, from Brando's point of view she also displayed, to use Brando biographer Stefan Kanfer's words, all the 'Brando requisites: lustrous eyes, an olive complexion and a reticent, almost virginal manner...' Or, as another Brando biographer, Charles Higham, put it, 'She was everything he desired in a woman. Her dark, glossy hair, firm breasts, and long legs excited him.'[6] Brando, evidently, didn't stand a chance.

Kashfi was ten years younger than Brando. Just twenty-

one years old, she had been in America for less than a
month. Newly arrived in Los Angeles and living at the
Carlton Hotel, she knew few people and on this particular
day was with Harry Mines (the Paramount publicist) and
A.C. Lyles, an associate producer on *The Mountain* who
had previously been director of Paramount's publicity department. Despite Kashfi later maintaining, 'No bells rang.
No glances were transfixed across a crowded room. If
bells had rung they would have been drowned out by the
din,' Brando's persistent stares apparently became so noticeable that Lyles left Kashfi to confer with Pauline
Kessinger who then introduced him to Brando, who in
turn followed Lyles back to Kashfi.[7] Writing about this
moment in her autobiography a quarter of a century later,
Kashfi chose to remember it thus:

> 'This,' I understood A.C. to say, 'is Marilyn Bongo.' Through
> the commissary noises and in the exotic environment, it
> sounded reasonable.[8]

She also insisted that she had no idea at that time who
Marlon Brando was: 'I had seen none of his films and did
not recognise him'.[9] This seems, frankly, impossible.
Brando, at the time of their first meeting, had already
made eight films including *A Streetcar Named Desire* and
Julius Caesar. And just six months earlier he had won his
first Oscar, at the fourth attempt, for playing Terry Malloy
in *On the Waterfront*. He had also won British Academy
Awards (as Best Foreign Actor) for three consecutive years
in the early 1950s. This was the era when millions of
people went to the cinema two or three times a week. By

anyone's standards, let alone an aspiring film actress, Marlon Brando was *famous*. Later that afternoon, Brando rang Harry Mines and asked for Kashfi's phone number. Mines, probably scarcely able to believe his luck, handed it over.

Two of the three people present the first time Anna Kashfi went out on a date with Marlon Brando have written about it. Kashfi claims responsibility for the presence of a chaperone: 'I considered it an impropriety to be alone with an "eligible" stranger, and I told him so.' Brando responded that he would be 'charmed' to furnish a chaperone. As Kashfi recounts almost ruefully: 'And he did. And we began.'[10]

George Englund, remembering Kashfi from that day in the commissary as a 'revelation out of Marlon's dream book, brown skin, lustrous eyes, fatal smile', agreed to be the chaperone.[11] Brando, dressed in a white shirt and white trousers, picked Kashfi up from her hotel in his black (or white – reports vary) Thunderbird, a present from producer Samuel Goldwyn following the completion of *Guys and Dolls*. His other car was a beat-up Volkswagen littered with old newspapers, hamburger wrappings and empty beer cans. The Thunderbird was for special occasions, he reportedly told Kashfi. The threesome ate lobster in a Chinese restaurant; Brando questioned Kashfi about India while Kashfi questioned Brando about America. Englund later recalled the evening as 'that funny and romance-filled first date when each of them wanted so badly to seem right to the other'.[12] He left before dessert and took a cab home while Brando drove Kashfi to his house in Laurel Canyon before escorting her back to her hotel later that evening. Whatever Kashfi felt that night, driving around the Hollywood hills in a Thunderbird with Marlon Brando and the whole of Los Angeles lit up in front of her, we can only imagine.

Their association didn't remain private for long. Word got out that they were dating, thanks to the efforts of Harry Mines, although it would be three weeks before the story hit the papers. And already there was the first intimation of something darker. When Spencer Tracy, wary of Brando's notorious reputation for seeing different women at the same time, heard that he was pursuing Kashfi he apparently warned her off: 'Anna, you're making the biggest mistake of your life'.[13] Nonetheless the romance would carry on (and off) for two years before the couple married in October 1957.

At first Brando's behaviour is described, by George Englund, as 'decorous' and the man himself as 'a little shy guy, a touch of European inflection, a soupçon of British good manners, no vulgarity, no Wild One'.[14] Kashfi herself said that after their first date they didn't see each other again for nearly two months; apparently embarrassed by not realising who he was she repeatedly avoided him. In his biography of Brando, Gary Carey maintained that the romance with 'this sari-clad houri' didn't become serious until Kashfi became ill with TB, yet all the biographers agree upon one thing – that 'Anna consumed him utterly'.[15] And they believed themselves to be privy to intimate details of their sexual behaviour. According to Higham: 'His need for her was absolute. They made love at all hours of the day and night, insatiably devoured by lust for each other's bodies.'[16] David Thomson recounted that: 'they became lovers and for a time he was infatuated with her, making love at every opportunity.'[17] While Darwin Porter decided that: 'Marlon's first seduction of Kashfi may have been tantamount to rape, as he picked her up and carried her into his bedroom without her permission.'[18] Kashfi herself is more prosaic: 'I went to bed with Marlon mostly out of curiosity.' She goes on:

> Marlon never phoned in advance of materialising on my doorstep, often at three o'clock in the morning. He rarely acknowledged the prefatory niceties of courtship (candy, flowers). After making love he could vanish without a word.[19]

Higham clearly felt the need to embroider Kashfi's account:

> Marlon would wake in the early hours of the morning feeling aroused, and, too impatient even to telephone her, he would drive to her apartment, ring the doorbell, and when she opened it, rubbing sleep from her eyes, carry her headlong into the bedroom and make love to her on the spot. Then he would leave without even saying goodnight. It was the most unromantic relationship possible.[20]

In post-war America, sex, like the economy, was thriving. Public Health Records between 1954 and 1963 showed that 82% of the population had had pre-marital sex by the age of thirty. And, of course, the controversial Kinsey Reports, published in 1948 and 1953, had already challenged beliefs about sexuality. Nonetheless, Kashfi's background, as a teenager in a Catholic household in post-war Cardiff, would have been far more sheltered. Remembering those years Kashfi admits, 'I didn't have a boyfriend, you know, nothing'.[21] But in Los Angeles she was learning to adapt, to play the game. In an interview with Hedda Hopper, in 1956, she said:

> Romance? This thing puzzles me in Hollywood. At home, I was usually chaperoned, but here I live like any American girl. I have an apartment alone and I have learned to drive a car. I date like American girls.

She was also lonely:

> Besides Marlon I knew nobody except Spencer, Katharine Hepburn, A. C. Lyles, Harry Mines and Harry Towns, all of whom were connected with the movie. It started off with holding hands. He was very concerned about me and what my feelings were. Considerate. Nothing kinky, nothing out of the ordinary.[22]

As their relationship developed they began to be seen around Hollywood at certain restaurants or, as Louella Parsons put it in her *Louella's Movie-Go-Round column,* 'Very quietly he's taking her to dinner at the less publicized spots and for long rides along the beach roads.'[23] Kashfi's professional life also expanded when, in December 1955, she signed a seven year contract with MGM. Louella Parsons broke the story in her Christmas Eve column:

I cannot remember when an East Indian actress has been signed in Hollywood. But Anna Kashfi, after an impressive colour test, was nabbed by MGM. Wonder why Paramount let her slip through its fingers? She is in *The Mountain* with Spencer Tracy and Paramount had first claim on her. But while the studio was making up its mind, MGM got her name on a contract. She has been called 'the Grace Kelly of India' because of her beauty and charm.[24]

No sooner had she been signed to MGM than Kashfi was loaned out (common practice within the studio system) to Universal to play opposite Rock Hudson in *Battle Hymn*. It's hard not to speculate that Kashfi's meteoric rise from a non-speaking role in *The Mountain* to co-starring with Rock Hudson, in a film directed by Douglas Sirk, within four months of arriving in Hollywood, had something to do with her promising relationship with Brando. Opportunities in films with big stars were highly coveted and the competition was brutal. Kashfi had no previous acting experience and no profile – apart from her association with Brando. As Dorothy Kilgallen in her *Voice of Broadway* column noted:

ANNA KASHFI, Hollywood's newest actress, is becoming famous out there just on the rumour that she's turned down three opportunities for a date with Marlon Brando.[25]

Esme Chandlee, the MGM publicist who had taken over from where Harry Mines left off, was apparently working hard on the same basis: dates or no dates, being around

Brando was like winning the lottery for an unknown actress. Working with Rock Hudson was also helpful. In 1956 he was approaching the peak years of his career and about to be nominated for an Oscar for *Giant* in which he co-starred with Elizabeth Taylor and James Dean. It was the last of the three films Dean made and he died before it was released. Working alongside Hudson, Kashfi was moving in illustrious circles. She and Brando, however, were about to be parted.

Committed to filming *Teahouse of The August Moon*, his ninth film, Brando left for Japan soon after Kashfi began work on *Battle Hymn* and the 'over-heated affair' was curtailed.[26] Higham noted that Brando 'hated to be without a woman in his life and greatly resented the fact she couldn't come with him' which is why, presumably, he invited his great-aunt June, his sister Jocelyn, her husband Eliot Asinof, and Phil and Marie Rhodes, a couple of old friends from New York, to accompany him.[27] Four months went by until the production, hampered by the rainy season, was transported back to Los Angeles – by which time Kashfi was seriously ill in hospital. After she finished work on *Battle Hymn* Kashfi was cast in *Ten Thousand Bedrooms* opposite Dean Martin in his first film without Jerry Lewis. Preparing to film in Italy, Kashfi underwent the standard medical examination required by the film's insurance company and was promptly diagnosed with pulmonary tuberculosis. In another of the strange coincidences that followed Kashfi around, the eminently forgettable, *Ten Thousand Bedrooms* went ahead without her and nearly sank Dean Martin's fledgling solo career – only for it to be resurrected the following year by his performance alongside Brando and Montgomery Clift in *The Young Lions*, the film Brando was making when he married Kashfi.

After the diagnosis, Kashfi spent a month in the newly-opened Mount Sinai Hospital on Beverley Boulevard (now called Cedars-Sinai Medical Centre) before being transferred to the renowned City of Hope Hospital in Duarte, some twenty miles northeast of Los Angeles on Route 66. By the 1950s America had TB under control; half a century earlier eighty-five per cent of Americans had tested positive for TB exposure but by 1960 the rate had fallen to five per cent, largely because of the discovery in the 1940s that antibiotics could eradicate the disease. However it remained the number one killer amongst the nation's infectious diseases. Vivien Leigh, born in India and rumoured to be Anglo-Indian, was first diagnosed with it in the 1940s and suffered recurrent bouts until it killed her in 1967 at the age of fifty-three.[28]

There is little doubt that Kashfi's lengthy period of ill health changed the nature of her relationship with Brando – or that it brought out the best in him. He became considerate instead of manipulative, arriving each day at the hospital with books, flowers, games and dolls. He set up a screen and a projector in her room so that she could watch 16mm prints of films – including his current favourite, *Singin' in the Rain*. According to Kashfi:

> Marlon grew more solicitous as my illness grew more serious. When I was on the critical list, his daily visits provided the succour, the emotional sustenance without which I would probably have succumbed.[29]

So smitten was Brando that he also narrated a documentary about the hospital, brought television sets for the patients and, on the days that he was filming, turned up in full costume and make-up (he was playing Sakini, an Okinawan translator) and entertained both Anna and the nurses. Despite this, Marlon watchers expected the romance to fade. Instead it grew more intense.

Meanwhile, there was no public mention of Kashfi's abrupt disappearance from the Hollywood scene and certainly not of her illness. She continued to be paid by MGM (but only because Spencer Tracy had intervened on her behalf) and the publicity machine kept on rolling...[30] Somewhat bizarrely, when Kashfi was seriously ill in hospital, the improbably named Franco Fatigati, an Italian pilot, was introduced as her prospective fiancé. Louella Parsons ran the following item, entitled 'Pilot Arriving', in her syndicated column in April 1956:

> Out of the blue, Anna Kashfi, the East Indian beauty, has declared a moratorium on all dates. The reason is that her boyfriend, Franco Fatigati, an Italian jet test pilot, arrives from Rome to see her in June, and Anna wants no local romantic entanglements to stand in the way of her romance with the pilot. When he arrives here it is possible that she'll announce her engagement. Her father, Devi Kashfi, an architect, gets here in early July to visit her, and that would be a very good time for her to tell the world about her matrimonial plans.[31]

In her autobiography Kashfi states that she was 'dating an Italian jet pilot' before she arrived in America – but *his* name was Enrico Mandiaco. There is no evidence that either of the Italians ever turned up in Los Angeles; no reference to Franco or Enrico visiting Kashfi during the months she spent in hospital. Still, the optimistic stories rumbled on. In May 'Actress from India', as the Oakland Tribune calls her, is expecting her 'young brother, Bosco, as well as her father as Hollywood guests this summer' (in reality, Bosco O'Callaghan, who was indeed Kashfi's nineteen-year-old brother, was working alongside their father, William O'Callaghan, in the Curran's factory in Cardiff). In June, the charade is complete when Louella Parsons forgets all about Kashfi's earlier 'moratorium on all dates' and, leaving out all mention of hospitals, declares:

> Ever since his return from Japan, Marlon Brando has been an every night visitor to the apartment of the East Indian beauty Anna Kashfi. You might say he has picked up where he left off before he went on location for *Teahouse of the August Moon*.[32]

One wonders what Kashfi, marooned in her hospital bed for months on end, made of these stories. Were they entirely the work of the MGM publicity department's Esme Chandlee doing her utmost to keep Kashfi's name in the public's mind so that her fledgling career wasn't snuffed out before it had barely begun? Or was Kashfi regularly supplying useful snippets which Chandlee then distributed around the Heddas and the Louellas? What is certain is that both the studio and the columnists, knowing that Kashfi was hospitalised with a life-threatening disease, could not possibly predict what the long term implications were for her career. Nonetheless, they colluded in their fanciful depictions of the imaginary life she was leading. Ironically, not much more than twelve months later, they would disregard the notion of fictionalising altogether and demand to know whether Kashfi was an O'Callaghan *or* a Kashfi – as if she could not possibly be both.

A year after Kashfi's arrival in America, in September 1956, Brando arrived at the hospital late one night accompanied by his close friend Carlo Fiore, an unsuccessful actor who was deeply mistrusted by Kashfi. After a rambling and sometimes tearful speech, Brando slipped his mother's engagement ring on her finger and proposed.[33] This was not the first time Brando had been engaged. In October 1954, a year before he met Kashfi, he proposed to Josanne Mariani-Berenger, a twenty-year-old French governess he had met in New York. The relationship fizzled out, apparently after Brando found out that Josanne had posed naked for a Polish artist, and by the beginning of the following year they had parted. Kashfi, like the French governess before her, duly accepted the proposal although her own account suggests she was not overly impressed:

> We had never discussed the subject of marriage. We had never exchanged pledges of commitment. Indeed, I had read in the gossip columns that Marlon and Rita Moreno were a 'hot item singeing the skirts of the Hollywood Hills'.[34]

Moreno had been in Hollywood since 1949, and would win an Oscar for her role in *West Side Story*. She was a rare example of a Puerto Rican actress allowed to play a

Puerto Rican character in the film. By contrast her on-screen sister, Maria, was played by Natalie Wood – an American of Russian descent. Moreno had an on-off affair with Brando for nearly a decade and when it finally ended, in 1961, she made a highly-publicised suicide attempt. For now, for the newly-engaged Miss Kashfi, Moreno would be just one of the thorns in her relationship with Brando.

After nine months in hospital Kashfi was released, on Thanksgiving Day. She went to the home of Brando's sister, Jocelyn, in Pacific Palisades, an affluent neighbourhood on the Westside of Los Angeles, to celebrate both the national holiday and her engagement. Kashfi initially got on well with Jocelyn, who would later say of her (Kashfi): 'She wooed me somewhat. She was beautiful, charming, graceful, winsome, really acting her part. She didn't seem phony at all. I suppose it was a campaign.'[35] Despite the celebratory atmosphere, Brando urged everyone who was there to keep news of the engagement within the family. Although he was known to despise the press and was extremely uncooperative with journalists, Brando's byzantine sex life – which ranged from one-night stands to overlapping longstanding, emotionally binding relationships – must have played a part in his nervousness about the news becoming public. His relationship with Movita Castaneda was particularly complex.

Kashfi was aware of Castaneda and dismissed her as 'a dark-skinned, high-cheek-boned Mexican several years older than Brando – six to sixteen years older depending on which studio biography is accurate'.[36] Castaneda had appeared in the 1935 film of *Mutiny on the Bounty* as well as *Flying Down to Rio*, the first Ginger Rogers and

Fred Astaire musical. She met Brando in 1952 while he was researching his role in *Viva Zapata* – the John Steinbeck scripted film about the Mexican Revolutionary Emiliano Zapata – and he was, according to his close friend Philip Rhodes 'absolutely smitten' with her.[37] Kashfi admits that they remained lovers intermittently for eleven years – 'at which time Movita became the second Mrs Brando.'

While Brando was living in his newly-acquired house in the Hollywood Hills above the Sunset Strip, Kashfi moved into an apartment block less than a mile away in West Hollywood. Brando selected the two-storey flat for her across the courtyard from where his father, Marlon Sr, lived. The two Marlons had a tempestuous relationship and during the ten months that Kashfi lived opposite him she spoke no more than a dozen times to her future father-in-law. In December, Brando again left Los Angeles for Japan to begin filming *Sayonara*, playing an American major who falls in love with a Japanese woman, a role which would win him another Oscar nomination. What Kashfi hadn't realised, until he telephoned her on Christmas Day, was that he had stopped off in Hawaii on the way. When she asked him what he was doing there he promptly invited her to join him and booked her a plane ticket under the name of Joanne O'Callaghan.[38] On arrival she had to wait for him at the airport for two hours and lost her temper as they were driving to the hotel:

I turned and slapped him, a fierce whack across his face. It was the first time I had hit him (or anyone). It foreshadowed many fights to come.[39]

Early in the New Year, with Brando finally installed in Japan, Kashfi attempted to get her career back on track after her lengthy absence. She had been cast opposite Glenn Ford in a slapstick comedy called *Don't Go Near the Water*. Unfortunately for Kashfi, Ford had fallen out badly with Brando when they worked together on *Teahouse of the August Moon* and his antipathy towards him extended to his girlfriend. A few days into filming, after a couple of unpleasant scenes, Ford took advantage of the casting approval clause in his contract and had Kashfi removed from the film. She was replaced by Gia Scala, born Josephine Scoglio in Liverpool to Irish-Italian parents, who later became a close friend of Kashfi's.

Kashfi was now back at home and despite receiving almost daily phone calls and a steady stream of letters from Brando, also read in the tabloids that Rita Moreno had followed him to Japan. When he returned to Los Angeles in mid-March bearing numerous gifts for Kashfi they became close again. It didn't last. Within a few weeks she felt that she 'could sense his affection for me shriveling.'[40] Again the Greek chorus of Brando biographers chime in with the same message:

> He was, apparently, no longer willing to commit himself exclusively to Anna, and Rita was as exciting and gorgeous as ever. He couldn't resist her.[41]

After she found Moreno's wig hanging on the corner of Brando's headboard, the couple had what Kashfi described as 'the first of our several pre-marital disagreements'. They broke up that night, only to get back together the following morning. And so it went on. According to Kashfi:

> Some of our breakups were occasioned by other women, some by senseless arguments and some by newspaper or magazine articles that accused Marlon of promiscuity, depravity, or some vague splenetic form of anti-social behaviour.[42]

Kashfi now began to be seen as culpable for the volatility of the relationship – at least that was the view taken by various Brando biographers. It is Kashfi who was described as 'fiery' (Higham), quickly roused to 'rages of jealousy' and a 'very difficult lady' (Manso).[43] Whether that was her natural inclination – or triggered by the circumstances she found herself in with Brando is impossible to say. Yet, what is clear is that however difficult she found Brando's relentless infidelities, she repeatedly returned to him. Manso described it thus:

> Being naïve and not terribly strong, she allowed him to reel her back in, thinking she had won the battle. Yet Castaneda was still in the picture too although, predictably, Marlon had not told her about his engagement to Kashfi.[44]

There was another hiatus in the relationship when Brando travelled to Paris in June to film *The Young Lions* with Montgomery Clift and Dean Martin. It was directed by Edward Dmytryk, who had given Kashfi her first role in *The Mountain*, and went on to be a huge box office success. When he wasn't working Brando wasted little time in becoming involved with an eighteen-year-old French-Vietnamese actress, France Nuyen. They had met the previous year and now, according to Higham: 'she fell hopelessly in love with him, never questioning his total dedication to her'.[45] Kashfi, meanwhile, had begun work on *Cowboy* for Columbia Pictures, on another loan-out from MGM. Her co-stars were Jack Lemmon and Glenn Ford – who this time didn't have casting approval. By late August, when Kashfi had all but finished *Cowboy*, and *The Young Lions* production company transferred from their French location to Borrego Springs in San Diego County, the couple were finally reunited. Kashfi moved into Brando's hotel where, as she put it, 'a quick sexual gratification, the consequences of which were nine months in development' sealed both her fate and her reputation as the woman who deliberately ensnared Brando once and for all.[46] Her pregnancy was described by Kanfer as her 'trump card' and engineered, apparently, because she was 'weary of his notorious affairs'.[47]

However, Brando, now aged thirty-three, far from feeling trapped, was intrigued by the prospect of becoming a father. An abortion was unthinkable. 'It's going to be my child too,' he said to Carlo Fiore.[48] This was undoubtedly a sign of the changing times. Although in America abortion remained illegal (apart from in certain states for cases involving rape or incest) until 1973, during the golden age of the studio era in Hollywood news of an illegitimate pregnancy would have destroyed both the star and her studio which had millions invested in her. Consequently, according to Fleming in his book *The Fixers*; 'In the 1930s, actresses routinely gave up unwanted children and abortion was so common that Marlene Dietrich described it as "our birth control".'[49] Publicity men, like Howard Strickling, concerned with the reputations of both stars and studios went to great lengths to conceal this form of 'birth control'. Abortions, and pregnancies known to be the result of affairs, went largely unreported by Hedda Hopper and Louella Parsons who were concerned with the film industry's reputation (and, no doubt, their own careers). One exception was when Parsons famously broke the story that Ingrid Bergman was having Roberto Rossellini's baby in 1949. Bergman was living with the Italian director Rossellini while still married to her first husband, Peter Lindstrom and the enormous scandal that followed Parson's announcement nearly destroyed her career. The Swedish star was ostracised by the press, denounced on the floor of the US Senate and exiled from America for nearly eight years.[50]

When Brando and Kashfi realised she was pregnant, they decided to get married – but were careful to not announce the pregnancy news until just over a month after the wedding and to always refer to the due date as July 1958. In fact their baby would be born exactly seven months to the day they were married. All three of Brando's wives were pregnant when he married them and he would eventually acknowledge eleven children, in and out of wedlock. But for now he was committing himself to Kashfi and told friends that he would give the marriage at least a year. He wanted, he said, to do the right thing for the baby.

Kashfi herself regarded their time together at Borrego Springs as 'the most tranquil and perceptive period of our relationship.'[51] But once they were back in Los Angeles, with Kashfi in her apartment and Brando in his house, the arguments began again. Rita Moreno caused a serious rift when Brando and Kashfi were woken up one night by her banging violently on the front door. Kashfi is said to have shrieked, 'It's her or me. Make a choice – right now.'[52] Despite Brando persuading Moreno to leave, Kashfi walked out and the next day returned his mother's earrings and other gifts. He brought them back the following day. 'We talked,' maintained Kashfi. 'We huffed and puffed. And, as usual, we ended with mutual pledges of devotion. Further, in this instance, we set a date for our marriage – within the following two weeks.'[53]

Notes

[1] Frank Morriss, 'Here There and Hollywood...', *Winnipeg Free Press*, 16 November 1955.

[2] George Englund, *The Naked Brando*, (Gibson Square, 2010), p. 43.

[3] *Los Angeles Times*, 26 June 1995.

[4] Ronald L. Davis, *The Glamour Factory: Inside Hollywood's Big Studio System*, (Southern Methodist University Press, 1993), p. 91.

[5] Anna Kashfi & E.P. Stein, *Brando for Breakfast*, (Crown Publishers, 1979), p. 54.

[6] Stefan Kanfer, *Somebody: The Reckless Life and Remarkable Career of Marlon Brando*, (Faber and Faber, 2008), p. 144; Charles Higham, *Brando: The Unauthorized Biography*, (New American Library, 1987), p. 165.

[7] Anna Kashfi, *Brando for Breakfast*, p. 13.

[8] Ibid., p. 14.

[9] Ibid., p. 14.

[10] Ibid., p. 15.

[11] George Englund, *The Naked Brando*, p. 43.

[12] George Englund, *The Naked Brando*, p. 45.

[13] Peter Manso, *Brando*, (Weidenfeld & Nicolson, 1994), p. 419.

[14] George Englund, *The Naked Brando*, p. 43.

[15] Gary Carey, *Marlon Brando: The Only Contender*, (Robson Books, 1985), p. 133;

[16] Charles Higham, *Brando: The Unauthorized Biography*, p. 166.

[17] David Thompson, *Marlon Brando*, (DK Publishing, 2003), p. 93.

[18] Darwin Porter, *Brando Unzipped: Bad Boy. Megastar, Sexual Outlaw,* (Blood Moon Productions, Ltd., 2005), p. 518.

[19] Anna Kashfi, *Brando for Breakfast*, p. 57.

[20] Charles Higham, *Brando: The Unauthorized Biography*, p. 166.

[21] Sarah Broughton, 'Unpublished Recorded Interviews with Anna Kashfi', April 2009.

[22] Hedda Hopper, 'India to Hollywood', 9 May 1956 (Margaret Herrick Library).

[23] Louella O. Parsons, 'Louella's Movie-Go-Round', *Alberquerque Journal*, 4 June 1956.

[24] Louella O. Parsons, 'Hollywood Scene', *The Stars and Stripes*, 24 December 1955.

[25] Dorothy Kilgallen, 'Voice of Broadway', *The Coshocton Tribune*, 29 June 1956.

[26] Stefan Kanfer, *Somebody: The Reckless Life and Remarkable Career of Marlon Brando*, p. 145.

[27] Charles Higham, *Brando: The Unauthorized Biography*, p. 167.

[28] Hugo Vickers, *Vivien Leigh*, (Pan Books, 1988), p. 8.

[29] Anna Kashfi, *Brando for Breakfast*, p. 64.

[30] Sarah Broughton, 'Unpublished Recorded Interviews with Anna Kashfi', April 2009.

[31] Louella O. Parsons, 'Pilot Arriving', *Waterloo Daily Courier*, 19 April 1956.

[32] Louella O. Parsons, 'Louella's Movie-Go-Round', *Alberquerque Journal*, 4 June 1956.

[33] Anna Kashfi, *Brando for Breakfast*, p. 72.

[34] Ibid., p. 72.

[35] Peter Manso, *Brando*, p. 420.

[36] Anna Kashfi, *Brando for Breakfast*, p. 44.

[37] Peter Manso, *Brando*, p. 310.

[38] Anna Kashfi, *Brando for Breakfast*, p. 78.

[39] Ibid., p. 78.

[40] Ibid., p. 87.

[41] Charles Higham, *Brando: The Unauthorized Biography*, p. 182.

[42] Anna Kashfi, *Brando for Breakfast*, p. 87.

[43] Charles Higham, *Brando: The Unauthorized Biography*, p. 186; Peter Manso, *Brando*, p. 443.

[44] Peter Manso, *Brando*, pp. 443-444.

[45] Charles Higham, *Brando: The Unauthorized Biography*, p. 182.

[46] Anna Kashfi, *Brando for Breakfast*, p. 96.

[47] Stefan Kanfer, *Somebody: The Reckless Life and Remarkable Career of Marlon Brando*, p. 157.

[48] Peter Manso, *Brando*, p. 461.

[49] E. J. Fleming, *The Fixers: Eddie Mannix, Howard Strickling and the MGM Publicity Machine*, (Jefferson, McFarland & Company, Inc.), 2005, p. 164.

[50] Jeanine Basinger, *The Star Machine*, (Vintage Books, 2009), p. 225.

[51] Anna Kashfi, *Brando for Breakfast*, p. 100.

[52] Charles Higham, *Brando: The Unauthorized Biography*, p. 189.

[53] Anna Kashfi, *Brando for Breakfast*, p. 103.

8

Years of Thorns and Vinegar

They were years of bitterness, of rancour, of temper tantrums: they were years of thorns and vinegar.

Anna Kashfi, *Brando for Breakfast*

Over Labor Day Weekend, at the beginning of September, one of the stranger incidents during those strange days reportedly occurred. Kashfi's imaginary father, Devi Kashfi, whose arrival had been regularly anticipated by the Hollywood gossip columnists, died. More than twenty years later, when Kashfi had long since acknowledged that William O'Callaghan was real father, she resurrected Devi Kashfi. She also altered her brother Bosco's relationship with her from brother to half-brother:

My half-brother, Bosco, called from New Delhi to notify me. According to Bosco he had been fatally shot; the body was cremated a few hours later without an autopsy. If Bosco knew more of the mystery, he wouldn't tell me. I never learned further details of my father's death. He was forty-nine years old. We had been close in spirit although separated by distance. He had telephoned me a month previous to advise me against marrying Marlon: 'He's a bum. I don't care if he's famous, he's still a bum.' I had slammed the phone down on him for his impertinence. Now I couldn't reason with him. He was beyond regrets.[1]

It's difficult to work out why Kashfi did this – perhaps Brando had suggested they visit her father after the wedding and she knew that would be impossible? Or did she think she was simply clearing the decks, removing all traces of her past life both real and imaginary in preparation for her future? Either way the extension of the lie is curious.

Just over a month later, on the morning of October 11th, Brando drove from his house in Laurel Canyon to a jewellery store in Pasadena to buy a wedding ring and then over to his aunt's house in Eagle Rock where he married Anna Kashfi. He wore that billowing black cape over a dark blue suit (with necktie), a cane and a black homburg settled squarely on his head, while the bride was dressed in an Indian sari. They must have been an arresting sight. The twenty-three-year-old Anglo-Indian actress dressed in a traditional Indian outfit, (although as Kashfi herself said, Anglo-Indians always wore 'European' clothes – they identified with the Anglo rather than the Indian aspect of their heritage despite living in India) and the thirty-three-year-old rebellious, anti-establishment, American film star dressed theatrically.[2] Two undeniably handsome young people, both in costume, both seemingly playing their parts in separate movies. After the ceremony, as he attempted to drive away, Brando told waiting reporters who asked him where they were going for their honeymoon: 'I have no idea myself where we'll stop,' and then added that he was 'very, very happy.'[3] Kashfi smiled and said nothing at all.

In the January 1958 edition of the movie fan bible *Photoplay*, next to a wedding photograph of the couple, was the following article entitled 'Love was Blind':

When she stood in her pink gold-embroidered sari beside Marlon Brando and took her marriage vows before the Rev. J. Walter Fiscus in the living room of Marlon's aunt, Mrs Betty Lindermeyer, at Eagle Rock, the girl who called herself Anna Kashfi was the happiest in the world. Now she may well be the unhappiest. William Patrick O'Callaghan and his wife, Phoebe, claim Anna is their daughter Joanna, not 'brown' as she stated on her marriage license, nor were her parents Devi Kashfi and Selma Ghose. The only point on which they agree was that she was born in Calcutta on September 30th 1934. A baptismal certificate was produced by a London paper to prove without doubt that the O'Callaghans were indeed her parents. Anna stuck to her story. And Marlon? Intimates say he is very upset, and think he did not know there was any doubt about Anna's being Indian. If there were, it might have dimmed her charm for him – he's attracted by all things Indian. Certainly he would not have permitted her to wear a sari – he's much too honest for that. It appears Marlon was blinded by the beautiful Anna / Joanna and she by her love of him. They'll have to open their eyes to the situation and face it honestly if their love is to survive its poor start.[4]

The Brandos were married on a Friday. The next day, Saturday 12th October, as they were on their way to Kathy and Louis L'Amour's ranch in Palm Desert, about a hundred miles east of Los Angeles, the story about Kashfi's disputed identity was front page news across Britain and America. As the paparazzi pursued them the pressure built with headlines like:

Britisher Says Brando's Bride Ex-Butcher Girl

Brand's Bride Welsh or Injun?

Joan Brando My Daughter, Says Welshman

William Patrick O'Callaghan Says Brando's 'Indian' Bride His Daughter

Brando's 'Indian Wife' May Turn Out Welsh[5]

Brando disappeared, leaving Kashfi to face questioning by producer friends from his production company Pennebaker – George Glass and Walter Seltzer – the same two men who had accompanied the couple when they drove to Riverside to collect their blood tests a few days before the wedding. Seltzer put it like this:

Senior didn't like her. He thought she was a fake, and after the story started to break, Junior despatched me and Glass to grill her. Marlon was very, very shook, and he wanted us to get to the bottom of it. His frustration was that he didn't want to be victimised. It was a question of control.[6]

Brando was also said to have hired private detectives to probe his new wife's background: *Who Set the Private*

Eye on Brando's Bride? ran the headline in the British Sunday paper, *Empire News*. Kashfi was, by now, 'all tears and hysteria' – not surprising given the effect of this unwanted attention on her relationship with Brando.[7] As for Brando himself, according to Stefan Kanfer, writing in 2009, this was his state of mind:

> Formerly he had been bedazzled by the costumes, sandalwood perfume and subcontinental aura of an Indian houri. When it became known that Miss Kashfi was one more pretender in a city of frauds, his interest rapidly flagged.[8]

The story, as we know, was rather more complex than the soundbite suggests. Kashfi was one of the hundreds of 'pretenders in a city of frauds' – as all the actors involved in the studio system at that time were. She was both a casualty of the double standards which operated in Hollywood and, most importantly, of her parents' own fractured relationship with their colonial origins. And as to Brando being cast as the apparent victim in all this – by the time of their marriage Brando had been in a relationship with Kashfi for two years. He had seen her passport, one supposes, hence his ability to book a flight for her on at least one occasion in the name of Joanne O'Callaghan – the same name MGM issued her paycheques in. And therefore his apparent shock that his new bride was related to someone called William O'Callaghan is puzzling. The mystery of her fictionalised parents, Devi Kashfi and Selma Ghose, is another matter, along with the bizarre tale of the murder of Devi Kashfi just weeks before their marriage

– but none of it is quite as straightforward as it looks. As Brando must have known.

When they returned to Los Angeles, Kashfi moved from her apartment into the Laurel View Drive house and, despite Brando's apparently 'flagging interest', he gave a succession of parties to introduce his glamorous new bride:

> Very nearly every major star in Hollywood came to their home on Laurel View; the Brandos were invited everywhere, because just about every woman in town wanted to see this mysterious 'Indian' Marlon had married.[9]

As the barrage of stories concerning her 'true' identity refused to go away, Kashfi maintained that Brando dismissed them as 'some garbage rooted out by a flock of vultures, when it blows over and the truth comes out, we'll sit down and have a good laugh about it together.'[10] In reality, the damage was done. Shortly after the wedding Brando reportedly said to a columnist 'I can't really talk to Anna. She is so emotional, so immature.'[11] This sounds highly unlikely given Brando's dislike of the press, and particularly of the Hollywood columnists, so it's safe to assume that someone in the Brando camp, Seltzer or Glass perhaps, planted the story in an effort to discredit Kashfi further.

A month later the pregnancy was announced: *Brando's July Baby*. 'We are very happy about it,' said Brando.[12] Kashfi's mother was also, apparently, delighted when the press told her the news: 'Marlon Brando's mother-in-law said today she was "very happy" the actor and his wife are going to have a baby.'[13] Meanwhile, the couple's troubles were escalating. Marlon Sr., acting as his son's business manager, attempted to supervise Kashfi's spending – which included 'a Rodeo Drive mink-shopping spree' with her friend, the actress Pearl Bailey – culminating in a huge row.[14] A few days later her publicist, Esme Chandlee, telephoned and heard her crying. She rushed over to the house to console her and then rang Hedda Hopper and put Kashfi on the line. The following day, in her column, Hopper made her feelings clear: 'my heart aches for this little girl. I don't think she deserves such rough treatment.'[15] Brando was, predictably, incensed. He and Hopper detested each other and he had already warned Kashfi: 'Reporters are all scum. Hired buffoons. Scribblers. Assassins.'[16] Now, more ominously, according to Brando biographers, he fell into a 'passive coldness'. In December, *Variety* reported that the couple had separated. Meanwhile Hopper was on the warpath making no secret of her intense dislike of Brando in a private letter to Jack Podell of *Motion Picture* magazine. She refers to her 'Brando Walks Out on Bride' article:

> I didn't want to hit him too hard in case there might be reconciliation. I don't think there will be, but there's always hope in the heart of a woman who loves a man even though he is a bastard.
>
> She's fallen down a flight of stairs twice because her pet cat goes down with her and got in the way. Her doctor was very concerned and said 'don't do it again – you might lose your baby.'

And then makes clear her opinion of Brando:

> Most people here just shrug off his behavior with the remark 'you know, he's crazy'. I think he's crazy like a fox and his bad behavior covers up his ill manners, inadequacy and belief that every woman in the world would drop dead for him. Of course he chose such a perfect time to misbehave – just as 'Sayonara' was being released. But he cares no more for a producer's investment than he does for his wife's feelings. He takes everything in his stride and don't forget for a moment this is a very sweet little girl and doesn't deserve such lousy treatment.[17]

The British press were as obsessed as their American counterparts by the state of the Brandos' marriage and on January 15th the *Daily Mirror* ran an 'exclusive' interview with Kashfi on their front page. Headlined *Marlon and Me* with a quarter page photograph of 'lovely Anna Kashfi', she was said to have 'welcomed' reporter Lionel Crane (*by-line: the only British Staff Correspondent in Hollywood*) into her home wearing a white dressing gown and scarlet slippers. 'Her dark eyes were sad as she said, "I wish people would leave us alone for a little while"'. After denying there was a rift between her and Brando, she said they were looking for a new house and, 'There is something else we must have too – privacy'.[18]

The issue of privacy in a business where people's careers depended on the lack of it was one taken up by *Movieland*, a popular American fan magazine, who used it to again speculate on the Brando's relationship in a piece entitled 'High Priced Privacy':

Marlon Brando and Anna Kashfi are having one of the strangest marriages Hollywood has ever witnessed. Ever since the holidays, Marlon and the dark-eyed beauty he wed last fall have been denying that they are having marital problems. Yet for a recent bridegroom whose wife is beautiful and intelligent, Marlon is hardly acting like a doting husband. Anna denied reports that Marlon has moved out of their Laurel Canyon home and that she was reportedly criticised by her husband for talking to the press. About this time, according to their friends, Marlon reportedly told Anna that he would like to be a bachelor on weekends and no questions asked. Meanwhile Anna, not wishing to displease Marlon further by discussing their marriage with reporters, had the telephone disconnected and is looking for a smaller place. Marlon's insistence on privacy in his personal life apparently is for real, and not just a temperamental gesture. It also carries a multi-million dollar price tag of which Marlon is well aware. 'How much,' he asked a veteran publicity man recently, 'would you say it will cost me to maintain this attitude on privacy?' The publicity man made an estimate that over twenty years, it might cost Brando between $5,000,000 and $10,000,000 in decreased grosses on his movies. 'It's worth it,' calmly replied Marlon.[19]

Kashfi did indeed find a new place to live. Brando suggested that she look for a Japanese-style cottage and she found exactly that at the top of Mullholland Drive, the road that separates Hollywood and Santa Monica from the San Fernando Valley. It sat in four acres at the end of a long private drive and the owner agreed to rent it to the couple for $1,000 a month. It was small, by Hollywood standards – two bedrooms, a maid's quarters, a living room, dining room and kitchen. Teak floors and white carpets throughout, chairs in orange Thai silk, Chinese missionary chests, wall hangings, a seventeenth-century Japanese screen and a carefully maintained water garden were all part of the deal. There was also a swimming pool. After the couple moved in Brando hung a sign on the gate: 'Unless you have an appointment, under no circumstances disturb the occupant.' He loved it and would live there, off and on, for the rest of his life. The move, however, did little to alleviate the tensions between them. Brando was rumoured to be seeing France Nuyen again, and Kashfi spent much of her time in the house on her own. In March her close friend Pier Angeli threw a baby shower for her and two months later, on May 11th, seven months to the day after her wedding, Kashfi drove herself to the hospital. At 7.30pm that night she gave birth to a boy, Christian Devi (known as Chris to his father and Devi to his mother). While reporters rushed to the hospital and the news was relayed around the world (*Marlon Brandos Have Son Born; Brando Father On Mom Day*) Brando waited until the following afternoon.[20] Kashfi said: 'Never had I seen him so emotional. For some time we were silent. Then he said, "The baby's wonderful – beautiful. Thank God he looks more like you than me."' The next day he returned to the hospital and assured her; 'From now on, I'll be a perfect husband... I'll love you... I'll love the baby.'[21] Despite these pledges Brando was already looking for an escape route – and trying to resurrect his relationship with Movita who was by then living in New York.

Kashfi admits that it was during this long and difficult summer, 'whether through self-pity or self-defence', that she first started using alcohol and barbiturates. She also admits to 'furious temper tantrums wherein I tore at Marlon's hair, threw dishes at him and assaulted his ears with obscenities.'[22] In July she spent three weeks in New York with Christian – and Brando seemed not to notice her absence. He was in pre-production on *One-Eyed Jacks*, a Pennebaker production, and held daily meetings at the house with the director Stanley Kubrick (Kubrick eventually left the project and Brando directed it himself). In late August, Kashfi went back to work on what was to be her final film, *Night of the Quarter Moon*. It was a controversial love story with the American singer Julie London playing a mixed-race woman married to John Drew Barrymore and Kashfi cast as Nat King Cole's wife.

Brando, meanwhile, was 'very disturbed, restless, and on a bummer' – for which Carlo Fiore blamed Kashfi.[23] A friend of Brando's, the actress Nan Morris, said 'Carlo used to say that she was the meanest bitch he'd ever met in his life, that "she won't stop until she's made everyone around her miserable"'.[24] It is the beginning of the transition of the portrayal of Kashfi from 'dark-eyed lovely' to 'bitch', the roots of which lie in the acrimonious disintegration of the Brandos' relationship at the end of the summer.[25]

The accidental and shocking death of their Japanese maid, Sako in September signalled the end of the marriage.[26] Sako, whose real name was Mrs Khasako Aizawa Milligan, was thirty-one and had previously worked for the film star Betty Grable. She drowned in the swimming pool in the garden of the Mulholland Drive house while

Kashfi and four month-old Christian were having an afternoon nap inside the house. A distraught Kashfi found her and, after trying unsuccessfully to pull her out of the water, called the police and fire departments, Brando's business manager, and various friends including Phyllis Hudson, the recently-divorced wife of Rock Hudson. In the ensuing confusion, the police believed it was Kashfi who had drowned and her death was announced on the radio. Someone called Brando; Kashfi explained what happened next:

> In the midst of the commotion, he walked into the house. He saw me and stopped abruptly. I can recall reading the emotions on his face: shock, apprehension, disappointment. 'Good God,' he spluttered, 'you're still alive.'[27]

According to Kashfi, it was the disappointment on his face when she realised she hadn't drowned, that ended the marriage. That same night she packed clothes, toiletries and personal papers into a case, tucked the baby under her arm and called a taxi.

Earle Hawley's article in *Photoplay*, '6 Days Before Love Died', described Brando's behaviour when Hawley arrived to interview Kashfi just before Sako's death. Kashfi was 'wearing white shorts, a green and white striped blouse and barefoot with her toenails painted with silver polish' while Brando was dressed 'casual-sloppy....in a short-sleeved knit t-shirt, dirty slacks and sandals.' Brando, with his baby son Christian slung over his shoulder, politely refused to give an interview and, after heating the baby's bottle, handed it to Kashfi. 'They both watched the infant until it was feeding contentedly and then Marlon excused himself and left the room.' Later, Hawley tagged along with Kashfi and the baby to the nursery and got a quick unofficial tour of the house:

> The dining room was small, with a very low table in the centre where guests kneel down to eat. The Brandos' bedroom was all done in mauve tones. The one striking piece of furniture in it was the large Emperor-size double bed, low to the floor, with a delicately carved, ivory panel fitted in the headboard. The nursery itself was a converted den where Christian was separated from his parents' bedroom by screens.

Back in the living room, Kashfi talked about how much Brando loved children, how they'd like to have more and about her loneliness when he was away. Hawley had the 'strange feeling that she was talking *at* me and not *to* me, that somehow she just wasn't there.' Later he described trying to write the story: 'The theme was always the same, the happiness of a wife and mother, but somewhere along the line something always went wrong. Little things Anna had said... and the memory of the expressions of sadness and strain that had flitted across her face...'[28]

On the morning of September 30th, Kashfi's twenty-fourth birthday, Hawley, still struggling to write his article, read the headline in the morning paper: *Anna Brands Brando Truant Hubby, Quits*. 'I can no longer take his indifference,' she said. 'I will charge desertion and cruelty.'[29] Six months later, in March 1959, Kashfi formally filed for divorce and was awarded a half-million-dollar settlement plus $1,000 a month child support. She was also got permanent custody of Christian with Brando permitted visiting rights of one and a half hours on alternate evenings plus Thanksgiving Day, Christmas Day and Christian's birthday.

The end of the marriage did not result in the end of the relationship. No longer sexual, it soon turned ugly with physical abuse on both sides. For the next thirteen years the pair were in and out of courtrooms fighting over their son until finally Kashfi, in a moment of complete madness, took Christian out of school and left him in Mexico with a group of people to whom she had promised $10,000 to keep him hidden. Brando flew back from France where he was filming *Last Tango in Paris* and hired a private detective who found Christian hidden under blankets in a tent in the desert. As a result Brando was granted sole custody, although Kashfi still had visiting rights. Two years later Kashfi married, for the second and final time, to James Hannaford, a salesman fifteen years older than her. Christian, by then fifteen years old, gave her away – while Brando had Hannaford followed for weeks by his private detective Jay Armes. The 'years of thorns and vinegar' didn't end there.[30] When Brando testified at Christian's trial for the murder of his half-sister's boyfriend in 1990 he said of Kashfi, 'She was probably the most beautiful woman I've ever known, but she came close to being as negative a person as I have met in my life.'[31]

Like every other public comment Brando made about the woman he met when she was twenty-one, married when she was twenty-three and divorced when she was twenty-four – it took place in a courtroom, under oath and at a time of great stress.

Notes

[1] Anna Kashfi & E.P. Stein, *Brando for Breakfast*, (Crown Publishers, 1979), p. 102.

[2] Sarah Broughton, 'Unpublished Recorded Interviews with Anna Kashfi', April 2009.

[3] *San Mateo Times*, 12 October 1957.

[4] *Photoplay*, January 1958.

[5] *The Daily Review*, 12 October 1957; *Tri-City Herald*, 13 October 1957; *The Salt Lake Tribune*, 13 October 1957; *Lowell Sunday Sun*, 13 October 1957; *Chester Times*, 14 October 1957.

[6] Peter Manso, *Brando*, (Weidenfeld & Nicolson, 1994), p. 463.

[7] Ibid., p. 463.

[8] Stefan Kanfer, *Somebody: The Reckless Life and Remarkable Career of Marlon Brando*, (New York: Faber and Faber, 2008), p. 158.

[9] Charles Higham, *Brando: The Unauthorized Biography*, (New American Library, 1987), p. 193.

[10] Anna Kashfi, *Brando for Breakfast*, p. 111.

[11] Ibid., p. 115.

[12] *Daily Mirror*, 14 November 1957.

[13] *The Lawton Constitution*, 14 November 1957.

[14] Peter Manso, *Brando*, p. 464.

[15] Hedda Hopper, 'Brando Walks Out on Bride Reports Say', *Los Angeles Times*, 14 November 1957.

[16] Peter Manso, *Brando*, p. 464.

[17] Hedda Hopper archive, The Academy of Motion Picture Arts and Sciences Margaret Herrick Library.

[18] 'Marlon and Me', *Daily Mirror*, 15 January 1958.

[19] *Movieland*, January 1958.

[20] *The ADA Evening News, Oklahoma*, 12 May 1958; *Indiana Evening Gazette*, 12 May 1958.

[21] Anna Kashfi, *Brando for Breakfast*, p. 124.

[22] Ibid., p.126.

[23] Peter Manso, *Brando*, p. 467.

[24] Ibid.

[25] Louella O. Parsons, 'Louella's Movie-Go-Round', *Albuquerque Journal*, 4 June 1956.

[26] Charles Higham, *Brando: The Unauthorized Biography*, p. 198.

[27] Anna Kashfi, *Brando for Breakfast*, pp. 133-134.

[28] *Photoplay*, January 1959.

[29] Ibid.

[30] Anna Kashfi, *Brando for Breakfast*, p. vii.

[31] Peter Manso, *Brando*, p. 982.

9

Plays Exotic

'She's my wife! I don't give a damn about the colour of her skin!'[1]
Franklin Coen, *Night of the Quarter Moon*

There is an interesting parallel to be drawn between Kashfi-the-actress and Kashfi-the-person. Kashfi-the-actress appeared in a total of four films between 1955 and 1959 – an unproductive tally by Hollywood's standards in those years. Her final role, in *Night of the Quarter Moon*, coincided with the break-up of her marriage to Brando. Subsequently, despite being less than half way through a seven-year contract with MGM, her film career abruptly ended. Although it was brief, Kashfi's cinematic sojourn is notable for the fact that she played as many different nationalities as there were films (Indian, Korean, Mexican and Angolan), and that each offers a glimpse of the world she unexpectedly began to inhabit. Her career is also notable for the impressive collection of actors and directors with whom she worked including Jack Lemmon, Spencer Tracy, Rock Hudson and Douglas Sirk.

Kashfi-the-person was an Anglo-Indian called Joan Mary O'Callaghan who changed her name and half-concocted an Indian upbringing complete with imaginary parents and an imaginary career in the Indian film industry.[2] She faked her biography. The dissembling originates from when she auditioned for the non-speaking role of 'Hindu girl' in *The Mountain*. By the time she played the Angolan wife of the African-American singer Nat King Cole in *Night of the Quarter Moon*, the world believed Anna Kashfi was the part-Irish, part-Welsh and by now estranged wife of Marlon Brando. She was personally castigated for apparently *pretending* to be 'exotic' while simultaneously *playing* 'exotic'. The fact that Kashfi *was* visibly, genuinely 'exotic' counted for nothing. She chose not to 'pass' as white, rather deciding to 'pass' as Indian. And so, although the answer to why she was *so* maligned does not lie in her film career, examining it offers an illuminating exploration of one aspect of Kashfi's life – and the business she tried to work in.

Kashfi's career as an actress began at the age of twenty. A sometime-model and shop assistant, a complete unknown, spotted by a talent scout (according to her), or recommended by a friend who worked for an agent – however it happened, after a brief meeting with the director and star of the film, she was on her way. When Kashfi arrived on set in the village of Chamonix, in the shadow of Mont Blanc, it is unlikely that she was aware of the complex relationship both the director, Edward Dmytryk, and star, Spencer Tracy, had with the film industry. Dmytryk, the child of Ukrainian immigrant parents, was one of the group of ten producers, directors and screenwriters who, in Cold War America, were given sentences of between six and twelve months in prison for refusing to answer the now infamous question: 'Are you, or have you ever been, a member of the Communist

Party?' Known as the 'Hollywood Ten' – they were in fact originally eleven – the writer Bertolt Brecht eventually testified but then left America the following day, boarding a plane to Switzerland before returning to his native Germany after fifteen years in exile. While in prison Dmytryk, alone of the 'Ten', agreed to cooperate with the House of Un-American Activities Committee in exchange for his freedom. He admitted to being a member of the Communist Party and gave the names of twenty-six people: six directors, seventeen writers and three others who, he claimed, were also members. Many of them never spoke to him again – and most of them never worked in the film industry again although some, like Dalton Trumbo, went on to write scripts under pseudonyms. Stanley Kramer, the producer who had launched Marlon Brando's screen career with *The Men* in 1950, was the first person to rehire Dmytryk. In the early 1950s he made a series of low-budget films. These were followed by the critically acclaimed *Broken Lance* which starred Spencer Tracy as an American cattle baron and Robert Wagner, born and brought up in Michigan of German and Norwegian descent, as his mixed-race son. Wagner's mother was played by the Mexican actress Katy Jurado. After Brando's death, Jurado claimed to have had a lengthy on-off relationship with him beginning in 1952 and, inadvertently reinforcing her connection with Kashfi, she also claimed that Louis L'Amour (the man who drove Kashfi to her wedding) was her 'true love'.

Tracy had given Dmytryk a script called *The Mountain* during the filming of *Broken Lance* and suggested that Wagner, who was thirty years his junior, play the role of his brother. They had become close friends with Tracy mentoring the young actor who would regard him as a surrogate father for the rest of his life. Like Dmytryk, Tracy was undergoing his own love/hate relationship with Hollywood. On the 25th June, some six weeks before he met Kashfi for the first time in Paris, Tracy was sacked by MGM after working exclusively for them for twenty years. He was in the middle of filming *Tribute to a Bad Man* (a forgettable Western which went on to lose more than a million dollars when it was released) on location in Colorado when the Studio decided it had had enough of the escapades of the fifty-five-year-old alcoholic and sent Howard Strickling to his hotel room to terminate his contract. Strickling had long referred to Spencer Tracy as a 'multi-problem person' and for years had operated what he called a 'Tracy Squad' to deal with him. Every bar, hotel and restaurant within a twenty-five mile radius of the MGM Studios had Strickling's private number and whenever Tracy turned up the 'Tracy Squad' were despatched to make sure that he arrived home safely. After quietly burying the news that Tracy had been fired, Strickling replaced him in the film with James Cagney. Tracy's illustrious career at Hollywood's biggest studio may have been over but he went on to make nine more films including *Inherit the Wind* and *Guess Who's Coming to Dinner* before he died in 1967. The first of the nine films was *The Mountain*.

Inspired by the story of Air India Flight 245 which crashed on Mont Blanc in 1950, French novelist Henri Troyat wrote *La Neige en Deuil* (*The Snow in Mourning*). Tracy loved the novel and regarded Troyat as a French

Hemingway. His representatives set up a deal with Paramount to make the film and Ranald MacDougall, a writer who had been Oscar-nominated for *Mildred Pierce*, delivered the script. The story was straightforward enough: Zachary Teller, played by Tracy, a gentle Alpine mountain guide, has a ne'er do well younger brother, Chris, played by Wagner. When a plane crashes high in the mountains Chris wants to climb the mountain to loot the wreckage and Zachary goes along with him to make sure he doesn't kill himself in the process. The victims of the crash are robbed by Chris while Zachary saves the sole survivor, a young Hindu girl (Kashfi) and brings her safely down the mountain. Chris, laden with stolen goods, follows them down and is then killed in a fall. The story might have been simple – but the location was anything but. No wonder Tracy was more concerned about how much Kashfi weighed than her acting ability – with altitudes of twelve thousand feet and regular two-hour treks up and down the mountain, it was a punishing environment to work in.

For Kashfi, her first experience as an actress must have been a daunting one. She arrived towards the end of August to find more than eighty people including fifteen from Hollywood, a French crew, six local mountain guides, forty-five porters to carry the equipment up and down the mountain each day *and* a cast of sixteen actors gathered in the foothills of Mont Blanc. And although what Richard Mealand had told her was true – that it was a non-speaking part and she needed only to react to Tracy and Wagner – it must surely have been intimidating. There was, however, no mention of any nerves in Kashfi's account – instead she remembered the difficult conditions, and Tracy's notorious temperament:

> Bad weather was responsible for endless postponements. Scenes were restaged from the peaks to the lower slopes. Still the funicular and the weather refused to cooperate. Tracy's celebrated temper boiled over with each perversity. Spencer was eternally a perfectionist. He would tolerate no laxity with me, with his co-stars – E.G. Marshall, Claire Trevor, Robert Wagner – with the director, with the technicians, or with the elements. When men or gods displayed a flaw, his rage could be volcanic.[3]

The conditions were indeed treacherous. One of the mountain guides, who also doubled as a stand-in for the actors, fell into an ice crevasse and his body wasn't recovered until the following spring. After this tragedy, and with the film nearing completion, the production team abandoned Chamonix for the less volatile location of the Paramount Pictures sound stage in Los Angeles. Years later, Dmytryk recalled the night before they left:

> On our last evening in Chamonix, the guides association threw a big party. It was quite a wingding, and, naturally, many toasts had to be drunk with the excellent local wines. Just as naturally, Tracy had to drink them. And so started my first and only experience with a periodic alcoholic.

The bender lasted for two weeks during which time the production was shut down, resuming after Tracy had been released from the hospital where he had ended up with a bleeding ulcer. Dmytryk was philosophical about it:

> Excluding the two lost weeks, the film was finished more or less on schedule, was beautifully scored by Daniel Amphitheatrof, and eventually released to a world that didn't really care to know why men climb mountains. It did quite well abroad, where Tracy was still something of a draw, but only so-so in America. Still Anna Kashfi got to meet Marlon Brando... and even Paramount didn't seem too unhappy.[4]

Kashfi appears only briefly in the film. Although her character is onscreen for most of the final twenty minutes she is only visible for odd moments. The rest of the time she is swathed head to foot in fur blankets with her face concealed as Tracy pulls, pushes and drags her sledge down the breathtakingly scenic mountainside. Despite this, it is still possible to glimpse what the Paramount executives saw when they signed her up. She is beautiful and she murmurs convincingly (Spencer Tracy explains that she's speaking in Hindi and that is why he, and he assumes we, can't understand her). Her eyes are startlingly expressive. She conveys alarm and apprehension certainly, but perhaps doesn't entirely enable us to imagine that she has survived a horrific plane crash. In her most dramatic moment, when Robert Wagner tries to strangle her to prevent his brother taking her off the mountain, she is not visible at all. But in her final scene we do see her face and her smile is radiant as she says goodbye to Tracy. What is most striking is not the performance – but how she looks. She has a bindi, a bright red dot on her forehead, her hair is long and black and gathered around her shoulders and her skin colour is undoubtedly 'brown' – the colour she identified as on her wedding certificate. She was an unusual sight in Hollywood films in the 1950s.

For her part, the job, the random casting as a Hindu in an American film shot in France, enabled her to escape – and to reinvent herself. Once she had arrived in the United States, her only contact with Britain, the country she had arrived in seven years earlier, would be an occasional visit. But she would not return to Cardiff and would not see her parents again. Now, it seems, the dissembling began in earnest:

> I had always travelled throughout Europe on an Indian passport. The United States, however, imposes a low quota for Indian citizens; queuing time for admission can extend to several years. On Spencer's advice – he had seized the role of my knightly champion – I obtained a British passport using my step-father's name, O'Callaghan. Subsequently, with marriage to Marlon Brando, the press uncovered this nom de convenience and concluded, with journalistic fervour, that I was an Irish lass masquerading as an Indian.

After stopping over in New York for three days, during which time Kashfi maintained that she 'shopped for my first dress, being accustomed only to saris', she travelled to Los Angeles.[5] Three months later, on December 24th 1955, Louella Parsons reported that Kashfi had been poached from Paramount by MGM – Spencer Tracy's former employer – and noted her 'Grace Kelly of India' sobriquet.[6]

By the time Robert Wagner escorted his new girlfriend Natalie Wood to the premiere of *The Mountain* in July 1956, on Wood's eighteenth birthday, Kashfi had made a second film and was midway through her hospital stay recovering from TB.

After signing with MGM, Kashfi was immediately loaned out to Universal Studios for *Battle Hymn* in January 1956 to play a mixed race, part-Korean-part-Indian woman called En Soon Yang. The part-Indian addition to the character was presumably made to accommodate the casting of Kashfi. The film was based on a true story about preacher turned fighter pilot Colonel Dean Hess who, after accidentally bombing an orphanage in Germany during World War Two, felt compelled to rescue South Korean orphans (with the help of En Soon Yang) during the Korean War. The script was flexible with the facts – and not least with Kashfi's character who was a fifty-year-old Korean woman (called On Soon Whang) but no matter: this was Hollywood and so the twenty-one-year-old 'East Indian' Kashfi played her. Rock Hudson was deemed rugged enough to play Colonel Hess in the film, which was one of nine films Hudson made with director Douglas Sirk. Hudson, born Roy Scherer, Jr. (his screen name was dreamed up by his agent Henry Willson who combined the Rock of Gibraltar with the Hudson River), had recently completed *Giant*, James Dean's final film, and *Written on the Wind*. Both would be major box office successes and catapult the erstwhile truck driver from Illinois to world-wide stardom. Hudson lived in fear of being outed as a homosexual – with good reason. Throughout the 1950s the noxious *Confidential* magazine had threatened to run stories exposing him. Hudson's agent, the ever resourceful Henry Willson, came up with a solution – he suggested that Rock marry Willson's secretary, Phyllis Gates. Gates apparently believed it was a love match and did not suspect that Hudson was gay until after the wedding. On November 5th 1955, the couple married and made sure that the first people they called after the ceremony were Hedda Hopper and Louella Parsons. A couple of months later Phyllis Gates struck up a friendship with Kashfi after meeting her on the set of *Battle Hymn* – and it was Gates that Kashfi would ring the day she found that her Japanese maid had drowned in the pool outside the house she shared with Brando. Gates divorced Hudson in 1958.

Battle Hymn is not ranked as one of Sirk's finest films. It is *Magnificent Obsession, Written on the Wind* and *Imitation of Life* which are critically acclaimed as subversive melodramas. The popularity of this last film was boosted by the real-life drama that beset its star Lana Turner when her daughter murdered Turner's boyfriend the year before it was released. *Battle Hymn*, by contrast, was not well received upon its release. *The New York Times* pronounced it 'clichéd' and Sirk's direction as 'obvious and mawkish'. Kashfi's performance was 'porcelain-like' – a description which feels somewhat harsh given that this was only her second job.[7] The fact that Kashfi received top billing after Rock Hudson – a significant step in an embryonic career – was also an indication of the plans MGM may have had for her given Hudson's

ANNA KASHFI

Exotic Anna Kashfi has been under contract to M-G-M for quite a while but she has made most of her pictures for other companies. Now she has starred in a film at her "home" studio, "Night of the Quarter Moon," in which she plays a negro girl. Anna was born in Calcutta and raised in Darjeeling and London. In her teens she studied pantomime and dancing, the foundation of Indian acting technique. This brought her to the attention of Indian film producers and later to Hollywood, where she has now made her home.

1. Constructing Anna.

2. First Audition, Paris, 1955.

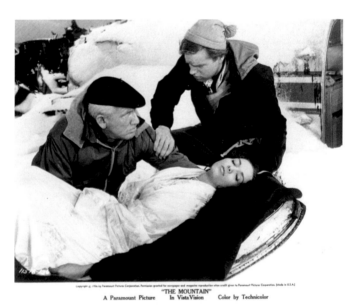

"THE MOUNTAIN"
A Paramount Picture   In VistaVision   Color by Technicolor

3. Kashfi, 20, in her first film, *The Mountain* (1955)
with Spencer Tracy & Robert Wagner.

4. Kashfi in her third film, *Cowboy* (1957) with Jack Lemmon.

NAME ____Anna Kashfi____ BIRTHPLACE __Calcutta, India__ BIRTHDAY _Sept. 30_

HEIGHT __5' 5"__ WEIGHT __110 lbs.__ COLOR HAIR __Black__ COLOR EYES _Dark_
                                                                    Brown

FATHER _Devi Kashfi_____ OCCUPATION _____ RESIDENCE _Deceased_

MOTHER _Mrs. P.W. O'Callaghan_OCCUPATION __Housewife__ RESIDENCE _Cardiff,_
                                                                   Wales

EDUCATED _Private tutoring at home; three years schooling at the French convent_

___in Calcutta; speaks fluent French, English, Hindu, three Indian dialects, some_
___Italian, Spanish and German; studied Indian art of dance and mime; studied_
___American tap dancing, etc._
MARRIED TO_____ Marlon Brando, Oct. 11, 1957._____

_____

_____

CHILDREN (Names & Date of Birth)   Christian, 1958._____

_____

CITIES LIVED IN _Calcutta, India; Darjeeling, India; London, England; Paris,___

____France; Rome, Italy; traveled around the world, throughout the Far East___

____and Europe extensively._____

STAGE AND RADIO EXPERIENCE ____None._____

_____

_____

5. Anna Kashfi's MGM 'studio bio', 1958.

'Is Anna disowning us?' ask the O'Callaghans

By GARETH BOWEN

WHAT is the truth about lovely Anna Kashfi, mysterious Cardiff-educated bride of Marlon Brando? In an exclusive interview today, I told Mr. and Mrs. O'Callaghan what Anna alleged in Hollywood late last night.

On returning from her honeymoon she stated: "William Patrick O'Callaghan, of Newfoundland-road, Cardiff, is not my real father.

"He is my mother's second husband," Anna added. "I was born in Calcutta to my Indian parents—Devi Kashfi, a civil engineer and architect, and Selma Ghose on September 30, 1934.

Legal name

The statement went on: "When I was 16 my mother married William Patrick O'Callaghan. I acquired their name and used it as my legal name on my first trip to England in 1952. I returned to India briefly thereafter, and then went back to London. My real father died only recently."

"Are these statements true?" I asked the O'Callaghans. Mr. O'Callaghan shook his head sadly, and his wife wiped the

750 stop work over one man's pit space

TROUBLE over one man brought the Fforchaman Colliery, Cwmaman, Aberdare, to a stop today when 750 men came out on strike.

The man, Mr. David Bailey, who lives in the Gadlys area of Aberdare, has refused for several days to work in a spot with only about 2ft. headroom.

A big-built man, he insisted that

6. The O'Callaghans interviewed in their local newspaper, *The South Wales Echo*, October 1957.

7. Dales Butchers in Cardiff where Kashfi worked as a cashier. The sign on the wall says 'Marlon Brando's Wife Worked Here'.

8. Belinda Lee

10. Gia Scala

9. Pier Angeli

first
photographs
of

MARLON BRANDO'S SON

Missing from these tender photographs of Anna Kashfi and her son is Marlon Brando, who has refused to share any family photographs with the public. Yet to Anna, Marlon truly lives in these photographs— for the eyes of Christian Devi, deep-set, dark and brooding, are Marlon's eyes. To this young mother who inherited the mysteries of the East from her Hindu father, a child's eyes mirror the soul of his father. Looking into Christian's eyes she sees again the man who—despite all—gave her an intense, wonderful moment of love.

Exclusive photos by Ina Berneis

11. Kashfi, 23, and Christian at the Mulholland Drive
house in the summer of 1958.

12. A 'bruised, barefoot and belligerent' Kashfi being arrested at the Bel-Air Sands Hotel, 1964.

13. 'Angry Anna'

14. Kashfi marries James Hannaford at the Dunes Hotel,
Las Vegas, in January 1974.

15. Author's grandparents, Ted and Jinty, on their wedding
day in Dundee, Scotland, July 1933.

16. Anna Kashfi's home, Alpine, California, 2009.

17. 'Meeting Anna'. Author and Anna Kashfi,
Alpine, California, April 2009.

box-office appeal at the time. Unfortunately, for most of the film Kashfi is curiously lifeless and not wholly believable as the one-woman powerhouse her character is based on. Once again, however, she fulfilled the brief of looking startlingly good on screen.

While the Anglo-Indian Kashfi was playing part-Korean En Soon Yang in Nogales (a city on the US side of the Mexican border which was passing for Korea), Brando, who was of German, Dutch, English and Irish descent, went to Japan to play a Japanese character named Sakini in *The Teahouse of the August Moon*. This custom – of white actors playing Asian characters – is now known as yellowface and is considered as offensive as blackface, but in Hollywood's heyday it was fairly common practice. Katharine Hepburn, Fred Astaire, Ingrid Bergman, John Wayne and Peter Sellers, as well as Brando, donned eye-pieces, rubber bands and make-up to play Asian characters – but perhaps the most notorious performance was Mickey Rooney's 'Mr. Yunioshi' (Audrey Hepburn's 'crazy Jap' neighbour in *Breakfast at Tiffany's*). Robert B. Ito in his article, '"A Certain Slant": A Brief History of Hollywood Yellowface' was scathing about the practice in general:

> During much of the so-called Golden Age of Hollywood, scores of actors, big-name actors, had no moral qualms about taking roles that required them to 'slant' their eyes, do that funny walk, and practice their embarrassingly poor 'Oriental' accents. Although most actors did the yellowface thing as a one-shot deal, a handful, like 'Charlie Chan' actor Warner Oland and Siamese king Yul Brynner, actually spent much of their careers unashamedly accepting such roles.[8]

Brando, at this time the number one box office star in America, received some six thousand fan letters a week and consequently could play almost any part that took his fancy. Fresh from an unhappy experience pitted as Sky Masterson in *Guys and Dolls*, the part he chose next was Sakini in *Teahouse of the August Moon*. The script was based on a best-selling novel by the prolific John Patrick who had recently adapted *The Philadelphia Story* into the musical *High Society*. *Teahouse of the August Moon*, about the post-war American occupation of Okinawa, had been a successful play on Broadway. As soon as MGM acquired the rights, Brando lobbied for the role of Sakini – the local man hired as an interpreter for the army captain tasked with Americanising the community. His co-star was Glenn Ford who, despite being on a roll with a recent run of successes – *Gilda*, *The Big Heat* (with Brando's actress sister Jocelyn) and *Blackboard Jungle* – received nothing like the star treatment afforded to Brando. The special handling included a salary of three hundred thousand dollars plus a further twenty-one thousand for each week the film ran over schedule. Only being required to attend costume fittings, photo calls, script readings and rehearsals one week before and one week after filming – and never working longer than an eight-hour day were also perks given only to Brando. It may have been Ford's resentment of the discrepancy in their status, or perhaps Brando's immediate dislike of him, which started their feud. Either way their mutual antagonism resulted in the socially conscious Brando and the conservative Ford openly fighting on the set – the consequences of which were eventually borne by Kashfi.

Following a month-long monsoon, the death of the distinguished character actor Louis Calhern and the incessant bickering between Brando and Ford, the cast and crew packed up and returned home to finish the film at the MGM Studios in Culver City on the outskirts of Los Angeles.

Meanwhile Kashfi, now embedded in the MGM production line, had been swiftly despatched into pre-production work on her next film following the completion of *Battle Hymn*. Her new leading man was to be the singer and comedian Dean Martin who, after his break-up with partner Jerry Lewis, was in search of the right vehicle for his first solo film. He turned down *The Pyjama Game*, a box-office hit, in favour of the limp comedy *Ten Thousand Bedrooms* which was described, unpromisingly, by producer Joe Pasternak as 'a sort of satire on the Conrad Hilton hotel chain'.[9] Kashfi was cast as a young Italian woman, Nina Martelli, proving once again that an 'exotic' can play any nationality, and began wardrobe fittings and preliminary rehearsals. As she prepared to travel to Rome, she underwent medical tests – standard procedure by the insurance company when a production was filming overseas. The results were serious enough to send her new life crashing into freefall. Kashfi herself described the diagnosis and its effect on her in her autobiography:

> Abnormal signs were detected, and I entered Mount Sinai Hospital for a month of diagnostic tests. It was found that I was seriously infected by pulmonary tuberculosis.

Blood-specked sputum, coughing spells, and shortness of breath are the symptoms of 'galloping consumption' as we called TB in India. In my mind I regarded it as a social disease; I felt shamed and remained out of communication with friends rather than admit my affliction. I confessed to Marlon only when I was removed to the City of Hope Hospital, a primarily terminal facility.[10]

As Kashfi languished in hospital, the twenty-year-old Italian operatic singer Anna Maria Alberghetti took on the role of Nina Martelli. *Ten Thousand Bedrooms* went on to be a disaster, both critically and financially – and 'almost killed Dean's acting career in one fell swoop.'[11] After returning from Italy Martin found time to host a nineteen-hour telethon, *Parade of Stars*, to raise money for the City of Hope Hospital. Although the stars included Sammy Davis, Jr., Perry Como and Edward G. Robinson, the show was panned by critics as a melange of third-rate acts, bad taste and bad grammar. Nonetheless, it brought in a useful $804,000 for the hospital. The telethon was transmitted on the last weekend of May – when Kashfi was a patient in the City of Hope – but there is no record of there being any connection between this and her one-time co-star Martin's charitable efforts. In fact, at this point, they hadn't actually met. Kashfi noted that, during her preliminary work on *Ten Thousand Bedrooms*, 'I never saw Mr. Martin at this time; his acting regimen excluded rehearsals'.[12] Their paths were finally to cross more than a year later when Kashfi joined Brando on location for *The Young Lions* in Borrego Springs.

Kashfi finally left the City of Hope hospital in November

1956. As she prepared to depart, out in the wider world Republican President Dwight D. Eisenhower was re-elected for his second term with Richard Nixon as Vice President and Britain, in the throes of the Suez Crisis, was rationing petrol again. Kashfi, newly engaged to a besotted Brando, was perhaps too preoccupied to notice the bigger picture. Now aged twenty-two and having spent months battling a serious illness, she was more than ready to kick-start her career again.

MGM was also anxious to have Kashfi back and to start realising some of the investment they had made in her. She returned to work in the first week of January 1957 following a turbulent holiday with Brando in Hawaii. Although she was later to dismiss *Don't Go Near The Water* as 'an unsophisticated comedy about Navy public relations' it was one of only three MGM films, out of the thirty-two that they released that year, to be nominated for Golden Globe Awards for Best Picture (the others being *Silk Stockings* and *Les Girls* – which won). It might have been 'unsophisticated', but MGM were keen to capitalise on the success of *Teahouse of the August Moon* (their highest grossing film of 1956) – and in particular the comedic talent Glenn Ford had displayed. The now long-forgotten *Don't Go Near The Water* was the first of several military comedies that Ford was to appear in. Kashfi, a mere eighteen years younger than him, was cast as his romantic interest, Melora Alba, a young native schoolteacher on an unnamed Pacific island. Still playing a one-dimensional 'exotic', yet still woefully inexperienced, Kashfi, having not worked for almost a year, was now up against a leading actor who she believed had a 'vendetta' against her new fiancé. It was a situation far removed from her first encounter on *The Mountain* set with the sympathetic Spencer Tracy and his close friend Robert Wagner – or even the polite, well-mannered Rock Hudson on *Battle Hymn*. As Kashfi was later to recall in *Brando for Breakfast*:

> He [Ford] flaunted his dislike for me early in the shooting schedule. In shots with his back to the camera, he would wave his hands in front of my face. In our close-up two shots, he would whisper obscene limericks in my ear. He never passed up an opportunity to carp at me: 'You're reading your lines all wrong... You're making me turn my wrong side to the camera... I warn you – I have casting approval.'[13]

The situation deteriorated rapidly. Kashfi sought advice from her mentor, Spencer Tracy, who suggested that she 'underplay' her performance believing that in acting terms less is always more. The following day she duly suggested to her nemesis, 'Mr Ford, why don't you underplay with me?'. According to Kashfi, Ford decided to exercise his casting approval immediately:

> 'You're out,' he screamed. 'Out, out, out.' He strode off the set. 'She's out, I tell you, out, out.' I was out.[14]

Her part was taken by Gia Scala who, as already noted, became a close friend of Kashfi's despite the awkward circumstances. Meanwhile, *Don't Go Near the Water* went on to make over a million dollars at the box office.

It's not clear exactly what Kashfi did for the next six months but by July she was back at work as Jack Lemmon's Mexican love interest in a Columbia Pictures western called *Cowboy*. This was Kashfi's second loan-out – a common practice at all the studios, as she was fast discovering. Every film actor's contract contained provisions that enabled the studio to assign them to any role in any film, no matter how inappropriate or mediocre, and also to loan them out to any other production company that would take them. This was how the studios attempted to control their 'fickle' actors, directors and any employee they considered valuable – being loaned-out was often seen as a demotion, a reprimand. It's likely though, in this case, MGM merely wanted to get some return on Kashfi to whom they had now been paying a monthly salary for eighteen months with only one (not very successful) film to show for it. Whether she wanted the part or not, Kashfi would have known by now that refusing to play a role, or declining to be loaned out, would result in suspension without pay. If even the biggest stars at the height of their fame often had no say in the roles they played, minor starlets like Kashfi quickly learned to both put up and shut up. Top box office draw Clark Gable once mentioned that he had never been asked about which parts he'd like to play and MGM punished him for what they saw as dissent by loaning him to Columbia Pictures for *It Happened One Night*. Ironically, the Frank Capra comedy went on to be the first film to win all five major Academy Awards (a feat unmatched until *One Flew Over the Cuckoo's Nest* forty years later) including Gable's only Oscar. Following this he signed a new seven-year contract with MGM in which they held exclusive rights to the use of his name, image, and voice. It also included a clause which stated that if Gable were injured or facially disfigured, the studio could suspend him without compensation. And when MGM's most popular and famous leading man asked for a percentage of the profits from his films a top executive was reported to have said 'He's nobody. We took him from nobody. We straightened his teeth and capped them into that smile... We taught this dumb cluck how to depict great emotions. And now he wants a piece of the action? Never!'[15] Otto Friedrich tried to explain the inexplicable – why famous, rich, celebrated people agreed to work under these conditions:

> They were frightened people, many of these famous stars, emerging from origins of poverty and conflict, driven onward not by talent or vocation so much as the simple hunger for what Hollywood could give them: riches, success, fame. (Lana Turner was surprised to realise, on making a count, that she had acquired 698 pairs of shoes.) And among the few who triumphed, and thus acquired a surrounding phalanx of managers, agents, publicists, paid companions, there remained always an element of panic.[16]

During the 1950s such draconian practices began to ease off – largely as a result of several celebrated battles between the biggest stars and their studios, including Marilyn Monroe. She was suspended by Twentieth Century Fox in 1954 for refusing to appear in the risible *The Girl in Pink Tights*, and, later that year, founded her

own production company. This act of mutinous and coura-
geous independence was instrumental in the eventual
collapse of the studio system.

When Kashfi was first offered the role of Maria Vidal
Arriega in *Cowboy* she told the producer, Julian Blaustein,
that the other male lead in the film alongside Jack Lemmon
had ejected her from her previous film. She was worried
that Glenn Ford might again have casting approval. 'Not
at this studio he doesn't,' declared Blaustein.[17] Fortunately,
Kashfi and Ford didn't have any scenes together and
managed to avoid each other throughout the production
period. Once again though, the still green Kashfi found
herself playing opposite an experienced star in Jack
Lemmon (he had won an Oscar for *Mister Roberts* two
years earlier) – albeit a more youthful one than she was
used to. Lemmon, only a decade older than Kashfi,
appears to have got on well with her – at least according
to Kashfi who maintained: 'our love scenes were so real-
istic that Jack's wife, Felicia Farr, watching from behind
the cameras, raised a fuss whenever the director called
for retakes'.[18]

Cowboy was written by Dalton Trumbo – one of the
Hollywood Ten now living in exile in Mexico and writing
scripts for a fraction of his previous fee of $75,000. In
1956, under the pseudonym Robert Rich, Trumbo won
his second Oscar for Best Screenplay for *The Brave One*.
His first was for *Roman Holiday* in 1953 – using a 'Front'.
'Front' meant that a friend allowed their name to be used
as the writer. For *Roman Holiday*, the English screenwriter
Ian McLellan Hunter obliged and for *Cowboy* it was the
American screenwriter Edmund Hall North (who would

later win his own Oscar alongside Francis Ford Coppola for the screenplay of *Patton*). In total, Trumbo wrote fifteen uncredited films between 1950 and 1960. *Spartacus*, for which Trumbo was going to use the pseudonym 'Sam Jackson', was the one which helped to break the blacklist when Spartacus himself, Kirk Douglas, insisted that Trumbo be publicly credited. Otto Preminger then announced that *Exodus* had also been written by Trumbo and thereafter the blacklist collapsed – although the recriminations within the film industry would continue for decades.

When Kashfi finished working on *Cowboy* she moved into Brando's hotel in Borrego Springs, a small desert town in San Diego County one hundred and fifty miles from Los Angeles where the dry, August, Californian land-scape doubled up for North Africa in the battle scenes in *The Young Lions*. This was the first time Kashfi had had the opportunity to observe Brando at work and she was impressed. She also discerned a noticeable difference in Dmytryk's attention to detail: 'Eddie Dmytryk had di-rected my first picture, *The Mountain*; I could compare his actions on that picture with the greater intensity he invested in *The Young Lions*'.[19] By mid-September both Brando and Kashfi were back in Los Angeles. It would be almost another year before Kashfi appeared in her fourth and final film.

In the intervening twelve months Kashfi married Brando and gave birth to her only child, Christian. The marriage, never stable, staggered along unhappily and Kashfi spent many months consuming a mind-numbing cocktail of alcohol and prescription drugs. In late August, when

Christian was a little over three months old, MGM once again came calling and Kashfi returned to work.

Her last film was, in retrospect, her most significant – for reasons that will become clear. *Night of the Quarter Moon* (also known as *Flesh and Flame* and *The Color of her Skin*) was the first Hollywood film not only to depict a mixed-race marriage, but also to make that marriage the main plotline. It was based on a true story about an infamous trial known as the 'Rhinelander case' which took place in New York in 1925. The case concerned a wealthy young white man, Leonard 'Kip' Rhinelander, who was persuaded by his parents to sue his wife, Alice Jones Rhinelander, for annulment and fraud. During the course of the month-long trial, which was front-page news every day, he alleged that his wife had misrepresented her racial identity. Alice Jones Rhinelander contended that the fact she was non-white was clearly visible and that, furthermore, she had never denied it. She won the case, but only after being publicly humiliated. In the courtroom she was forced to expose parts of her shoulder and her thighs to the judge and jury so that they could assess that she was indeed, visibly, mixed-race. The case rested on the fact that, as it was proven that Alice and Kip had had sex before their marriage (also controversial in 1925), then Kip *must* have known she had 'nonwhite ancestry'.[20]

Over thirty years later, *Night of the Quarter Moon* relocated the story to present-day San Francisco and cast the 'lightly tanned' Californian-born singer Julie London (real name Nancy Peck), best known for her hit song, *Cry Me a River*, as Ginny O'Sullivan Nelson (Alice Jones Rhinelander). John Drew Barrymore played Roderick

'Chuck' Nelson (Kip Rhinelander) and Kashfi was cast as Maria Robben, Ginny's cousin from the 'Angolan side' of the family and an 'exotic dancer' married to a piano-playing Cy Robben, played by Nat King Cole.[21] Kashfi maintains that she was originally cast as Louis Armstrong's daughter until he was replaced by Nat King Cole and she was then 'elevated to the rank of wife'.[22]

The film departs from the original case, and perhaps demonstrates the passage of time in American race relations, in that, where the real Alice Jones Rhinelander was ambiguous about her father's origins (in the sense that she knew there was 'nonwhite ancestry' in her family and told her prospective husband – but was not sure where it came from) in the film both Ginny and Chuck are fully aware of her black ancestry. Indeed Chuck is portrayed as being completely unperturbed by this until he eventually succumbs to pressure from his parents. As Heidi Ardizzone points out, *Night of the Quarter Moon* 'represented a significant transitional moment between the "passing" films of the late 1940s and 1950s and the films of the late 1960s usually cited as the first treatments of interracial marriage.'[23] The subject matter, however, remained as contentious as it had been in the 1920s – a fact borne out by a 1958 Gallop poll stating that 94% of white Americans disapproved of interracial marriage. Nearly a decade later *Guess Who's Coming to Dinner*, starring Spencer Tracy and Katharine Hepburn, would still be considered extremely controversial for featuring a relationship between a black man (Sidney Poitier) and a white woman (Katherine Houghton – Hepburn's niece in real-life). Attitudes had been changing, albeit slowly, since the end of World War Two. California, for instance, re-pealed its anti-miscegenation law in 1948 (fortunately for Kashfi and Brando or, nine years later, they would have been unable to marry in the city in which they lived) and by the 1960s, civil rights organisations were helping interracial couples who were being penalised for their re-lationships take their cases to the Supreme Court. Six months before *Guess Who's Coming to Dinner* was released in December 1967, the seventeen remaining American States where anti-miscegenation laws were still legal were forced to remove them after Richard and Mildred Loving famously won their case at the US Supreme Court.

In the 1950s the cinematic trailer for *Night of the Quarter Moon* felt it necessary to forewarn audiences about the controversial nature of the film:

It's the taboo theme for the first time![24]

And, unsurprisingly, Kashfi, was troubled by her part in the film:

My role was that of the girl's cousin, married to nightclub owner Nat King Cole. (In the original version I was to play the daughter to Louie [sic] Armstrong; but when he was replaced by Nat, I was elevated to the rank of wife.) I experienced some difficulty with the part because of a close identification with the racial theme. As before, Spencer Tracy's encouragement and instruction helped in repressing my personal reactions. 'Don't fret about it,' he said, 'acting doesn't require much brainpower – look at your husband.'[25]

Kashfi was also, reportedly, appalled by the courtroom scene where Ginny is instructed to disrobe. According to *Los Angeles Mirror-N News*:

> Anna Kashfi, who portrayed 'Maria,' protested this scene as it was filmed and ran from the stage 'in hysterics.' Kashfi stated, 'It's humiliating. I am not a Negro but what they are doing is exploiting the race.' Kashfi, according to the article, was forced to return, and though she expressed the wish to leave the project, director Hugo Haas said that would be impossible.[26]

In the film there is a scene between Ginny and Maria where Maria warns her about 'white people':

> A lot of them are nice. They're friends with you. They give you jobs. They even go to bed with you. But just don't try to marry into the family.[27]

Maria also gives her cousin Ginny advice which, for Kashfi, must have resonated with her own recent experience with her parents:

> When you have one little drop of African blood in you, just one little drop and they find out, you're a Negro.[28]

William O'Callaghan's resolute assertion to the world's press less than a year earlier, 'There is no Indian blood in our family,' must have felt doubly incongruous given that Kashfi, manifestly, had at least 'one little drop' of something which made her mixed-race – and furthermore chose to connect wholeheartedly with that part of her identity.[29]

In another scene, this time with Chuck, where Maria and Cy try to explain what it is like to live as non-whites in a racist America, Maria points out that she, as a light-skinned person, might have tried to 'pass' but she grew up watching her mother work as a maid for whites:

We call it the black curtain. There are some people who sneak behind it, some who sneak back away from it, and others who try to make believe it doesn't even exist. But it does Chuck, and like it or not you're on one side and Ginny's on the other.[30]

In 1948, a decade before he played Kashfi's husband in *Night of the Quarter Moon*, Nat King Cole had direct experience of America's racism when he bought a house in a previously exclusively white neighbourhood of Los Angeles. The Klu Klux Klan, who remained active in Los Angeles well into the 1950s, burned the N-word into his lawn and poisoned his dog. In the film, as Cy, Nat King Cole asks Chuck, 'Does the colour of her skin really make that much difference? Why does life have to be like this?'[31]

Night of the Quarter Moon's ending differed from the real-life Rhinelander case. The film version was given a positive Hollywood-style happy-ever-after-ending with a reunited Chuck and Ginny driving off, literally, into the sunset. For the real-life Alice and Kip life was bleak. Neither remarried and Kip died at the age of thirty-two. *Night of the Quarter Moon* was ahead of its time in its depiction of a mixed-race marriage and laid the foundations for the much heralded *Guess Who's Coming to Dinner* – although as Heidi Ardizzone points out:

> By 1959, Hollywood was ready to make a film about a marriage between a black person who did not deny having black ancestry, and a white person who knew his or her spouse was not white. But audiences were not yet ready.[32]

The critics gave it a mixed reception. The *Los Angeles Times* decided that the film 'has its heart in all the right places' but:

> Good grief the script isn't anywhere close to the weight sufficient to carry the burden of such a drama or of such a message as that of justice and human maturity and basic intelligence among the races of man. 'Quarter Moon' is, alas, but a fourth of a picture.[33]

He went on to pay Kashfi a back-handed compliment: 'Miss Kashfi's technique is still imperfect but she has style.' And with that the 'Grace Kelly of India's' career in films ended – not with a bang but a whimper.[34] Over the ensuing years no one ever remembered her for the roles she played on screen. Unfortunately, compared to the real-life ongoing drama provided by her fifteen-year battle with Brando over their child, her film roles paled into insignificance.

Notes

[1] Franklin Coen, *Night of the Quarter Moon*, front cover.

[2] Harry Mines, Paramount Studio Biography of Anna Kashfi, September 1955.

[3] Anna Kashfi & E.P. Stein, *Brando for Breakfast*, (Crown Publishers, Inc., 1979), p. 19.

[4] Edward Dmytryk, *It's A Hell Of A Life But Not A Bad Living: A Hollywood Memoir*, (Times Books, 1978), p. 205.

[5] Anna Kashfi, *Brando for Breakfast*, p. 20.

[6] Louella O. Parsons, 'Hollywood Scene', *The Stars and Stripes*, 24 December 1955.

[7] *The New York Times*, 16 February 1957.

[8] Robert B. Ito, '"A Certain Slant": A Brief History of Yellowface', *Bright Lights Film Journal*, 2 May 2014.

[9] Nick Tosches, *Dino* (Vintage 1999), p. 294.

[10] Anna Kashfi, *Brando for Breakfast*, p. 64.

[11] Nick Tosches, *Dino*, p. 298.

[12] Anna Kashfi, *Brando for Breakfast*, p. 63.

[13] Ibid., p. 79.

[14] Ibid., p. 79.

[15] Jeanine Basinger, *The Star Machine*, (Vintage Books, 2009), p. 141.

[16] Otto Friedrich, *City of Nets: A Portrait of Hollywood in the 1940s,* (Harper & Row, 1986), p. 193.

[17] Anna Kashfi, *Brando for Breakfast*, p. 90.

[18] Ibid., p. 91.

[19] Ibid., p. 98.

[20] Heidi Ardizzone, 'Catching Up with History: *Night of the Quarter Moon*, the Rhinelander Case, and Interracial Marriage in 1959' in Camilla Fojas and Mary Beltran, eds., *Mixed Race Hollywood* (New York University Press, 2008), pp. 87-112.

[21] Ibid.

[22] Anna Kashfi, *Brando for Breakfast*, p. 131.

[23] Heidi Ardizzone, 'Catching Up with History: *Night of the Quarter Moon*, the Rhinelander Case, and Interracial Marriage in 1959, p. 90.

[24] Script for trailer, *Night of the Quarter Moon*, Metro-Goldwyn-Mayer, 1959.

[25] Anna Kashfi, *Brando for Breakfast*, p. 131.

[26] *Los Angeles Mirror-News*, 11 September 1958.

[27] Frank Davis and Franklin Coen, *Night of the Quarter Moon*, Metro-Goldwyn-Mayer, 1959.

[28] Ibid.,

[29] *The Times*, 13 October 1957.

[30] Frank Davis and Franklin Coen, *Night of the Quarter Moon*, Metro-Goldwyn-Mayer, 1959.

[31] Ibid.

[32] Heidi Ardizzone, 'Catching Up with History: *Night of the Quarter Moon*, the Rhinelander Case, and Interracial Marriage in 1959, pp. 102-103.

[33] Charles Stinson, *Los Angeles Times*, 3 April 1959.

[34] Louella O. Parsons, 'Hollywood Scene', *The Stars and Stripes*, 24 December 1955.

10

Valley of the Dolls

You've got to climb to the top of Mount Everest to reach the Valley of the Dolls. It's a brutal climb to reach that peak, which so few have seen. You never knew what was really up there, but the last thing you expected to find was the Valley of the Dolls. You stand there, waiting for the rush of exhilaration you thought you'd feel – but it doesn't come. You're too far away to hear the applause and take your bows. And there's no place left to climb. You're alone, and the feeling of loneliness is overpowering. The air is so thin you can scarcely breathe. You've made it – and the world says you're a hero. But it was more fun at the bottom when you started, with nothing more than hope and the dream of fulfilment. All you saw was the top of that mountain – there was no-one to tell you about the Valley of the Dolls. But it's different when you reach the summit. The elements have left you battered, deafened, sightless – and too weary to enjoy your victory.[1]

Jacqueline Susann, *Valley of the Dolls*

When Jacqueline Susann was going through one of the many rewrites on *Valley of the Dolls*, before its publication in 1966, there was a suggestion that she change the ending which was considered 'dreary' and 'such a downer'.[2] Susann was having none of it:

149

'I'm not going to put a fucking happy ending on this book,' she said. 'That's not the way life works for these people. These are people who have bad lives, whose lives are screwed up by pills and the kind of pressure that show business puts on them, by the buying and selling of "meat" in the world they live in. It does this to them.'[3]

The *people* Susann refers to are her main characters Anne Welles, Neeley O'Hara and Jennifer North: three young women who become friends while trying to make careers for themselves in the entertainment industry. Susann herself was a bit-part actress in the 1940s and 50s and knew the business well enough – even if her fame as a writer far surpassed any success she had in her performing career. Susann's pioneering approach to getting her book into the coveted number one slot on the best-seller list changed how publishers promoted their wares forever after her relentless sales campaign propelled *Valley of the Dolls* into becoming the most popular novel in the world in the late 1960s.[4] It was a book that aroused strong feelings amongst its critics: even Gloria Steinem, who championed it for turning non-readers into readers, said that, 'compared to Jacqueline Susann, Harold Robbins writes like Proust'.[5] Over the past half century there has been much speculation as to which real-life stars inspired Susann's female protagonists. According to her biographer, Barbara Seaman, Neeley was Judy Garland and Anne was a composite of three women including Susann herself, her mother – and, Susann sometimes implied, Grace Kelly. Jennifer North was assumed to have been the 'Marilyn Monroe' character but actually bore a closer resemblance to Susann's close friend and lover Carole Landis, a contract player who ricocheted between the studios before acquiring the acronym 'The Ping Girl'. Landis was so angry with this nonsensical label (*The Ping Girl of America – because she wants to purr*) that she took out an advert in *Variety* protesting 'this mental blitzkreig'.[6] She appeared in a total of fifty-four films in her eleven-year career before committing suicide at the age of twenty-nine in 1948 in the midst of a turbulent relationship with the married British actor Rex Harrison.

Susann, after an unsuccessful career as an actress, was driven by the ambition to become a best-selling writer after being diagnosed with cancer. She wrote a paean to the young women like herself who dared to dream that a career in show business offered them an escape route from who they were but then found themselves washed up, rinsed out and left to hang. Julie Burchill, in typically Burchillian fashion, said the following in her introduction to the Virago edition of *Valley of the Dolls*:

> Hence her book is not a Sixties feminist novel, thank God, in the tradition of such souped-up, dressed-down sob sisters as Doris Lessing, Margaret Drabble and Edna O'Brien, who also wrote of young women with an ambitious energy which, due to the stonking gender inequality of the time, they ended up frittering away on destructive love.

In Burchill's opinion it remains a 'brave, bold, angry and, yes, definitely a feminist book.'[7]

As a cautionary tale, *Valley of the Dolls* arrived too late for Anna Kashfi. Aged thirty-one, she was a decade away from George Englund's exuberant memory of that first date: 'Marlon and Anna were happy; they were beautiful and so pleased to be with each other' and now found herself ensconced deep within the *Valley of the Dolls*.[8] Jacqueline Susann called pills *dolls* and wrote the book to warn people about how dangerous they were: 'Pills aren't taken to escape reality at first. They're taken so a person can cope with reality.' In fact, in *Valley of the Dolls*, 'dolls' had two different meanings:

> On one level the 'dolls' of the title are the pills that, like childhood toys, lull the heroines to sleep and then pep them up for the new day. On another level, of course, the dolls are the heroines themselves, whose stories intertwine over a twenty-year period beginning just after World War II.[9]

Three young women, all contemporaries and friends of Kashfi's who became, to quote Susann's words again, 'battered, deafened, sightless' provide a context for Kashfi's early adult life. They illuminate the chaotic, destructive milieu inhabited by Kashfi and other starlets, a milieu which many did not survive. Belinda Lee, Pier Angeli and Gia Scala were film actresses who teetered on the brink of major stardom. How they became actors, the parts they played, the way their careers ended – and the ways *they* ended provide fleeting glimpses into Kashfi's world.

Although Lee, Angeli and Scala made a total of seventy-one films between them, less than a handful are remembered today. Their careers were disjointed and their legacies fragmentary unlike, say, Veronica Lake, Lauren Bacall and Barbara Stanwyck, who mined distinctive and iconic seams. Bacall, Stanwyck and Lake also got decent roles in decent films – Lee, Angeli and Scala were seldom given the opportunity to reveal the depths of their talent, Scala in *The Guns of Navarone* and Angeli in *Somebody Up There Likes Me* being rare exceptions. They also embody different aspects of Kashfi's own fate. Angeli's unhappy marriage to a well-known personality was played out in the full glare of studio-generated publicity, as were the bitter custody battles over their son, which mirrored Kashfi's experiences with Brando. And both Lee and Scala were young British-born women who, like Kashfi, found themselves in California in pursuit of careers in the film business. Unlike Kashfi, all three were to die horrible deaths before the age of forty.

Belinda Lee was summed up by Matthew Sweet in *Shepperton Babylon* thus:

> A hotelier's daughter from Budleigh Salterton who lent a disproportionately Amazonian presence to a number of middling Rank comedies, before becoming a heroine of European pulp cinema, signing a suicide pact with an Italian prince and dying in a car crash in 1961.[10]

The brevity of Sweet's résumé does Lee a disservice. She was, undoubtedly, a conspicuously striking young woman but one who rebelled against the 'dumb blonde' roles she played in now obscure post-war British films.[11] Diana Dors, four years older than Lee and her closest rival in those Rank starlet days, is the name that survives – yet Lee's career is, arguably, more interesting and the risks she took more dramatic.

Belinda Lee, nine months younger than Anna Kashfi, was born in Budleigh Salterton, a sleepy coastal resort town in Devon in 1935. Her ex-army captain father owned the popular Rosemullion Hotel and her mother was a florist. The Lees were clearly a family of some means and sent their daughter to Rookesbury Park Preparatory School in Hampshire. By the age of nine, she was back in Devon as a boarder at St Margaret's School in Exeter, some fifteen miles from Budleigh Salterton. It was 1944 and Exeter, one of the Cathedral cities high on the list of targets for the Luftwaffe's 'Baedeker raids' (named after the famous German travel guides), had been repeatedly bombed.[12] Further down the coast, a large Royal Marine Training camp housing more than five thousand people was established on East Budleigh Common just outside Lee's home town. Despite the somewhat surreal rubble-strewn surroundings Billie, as Lee was now known, thrived in her new school and developed a passion for theatre. Three years later, just as Kashfi's family were preparing to emigrate from India to Britain, twelve-year-old Lee went to stage school, enrolling at the Tudor Arts Academy in Surrey. Later still, after her parents' divorce, Lee moved again – this time to London where she and her mother began a new life in South Kensington.

In 1952, and by now seventeen, Lee won a scholarship to the Royal Academy of Dramatic Art (RADA). It was during this period that she shared a flat with Kashfi. During her summer break from drama school, she kick-started her acting career by appearing at Nottingham Playhouse in *The Skin Game* and *As You Like It*. The following year, while still at RADA, she met the film producer Val Guest at a party, and was offered a cameo role in Frankie Howerd's film debut *The Runaway Bus*. Despite, apparently, preferring Shakespeare Lee left RADA and signed a contract with Rank Studios. She was memorable as one of the schoolgirls in *The Belles of St Trinian's* and then played a succession of 'dumb blondes' in middling British comedies alongside Norman Wisdom and Benny Hill. When she was finally offered something of more substance – a non-comedic role in the thriller *Eyewitness* – the reviews were underwhelming. *Picturegoer* magazine was damning in its faint praise: 'Belinda Lee doesn't come off so well in a uniform, as a conventionally cosy nurse, although it's remarkable how she brings lustre to any old role these days.'[13] This was followed by 'sexy barmaid' Gloria in *The Big Money* opposite Ian Carmichael (which Diana Dors had already turned down). It signalled the end of Lee's 'dumb blonde roles'.

In 1954, when she was nineteen, Lee met and married the stills photographer Cornel Lucas and they worked hard as a couple to promote her career with Lucas apparently sending out ten thousand pictures of her to magazines around the world. Despite this dedication the relationship faltered and three years later Lee declared,

> Our marriage is over. I'm very sorry, but I can't keep on living with a man I don't love. I'm ambitious and I want to be an international star and it's impossible to combine marriage and ambition.[14]

In fact she was by now pursuing a very public affair with a married Italian aristocrat called Prince Filippo Orsini. Orsini was a war hero and, to complicate matters further, the Assistant to the Papal Throne. In post-war Catholic Italy, Orsini and Lee's behaviour was considered outrageous. The Pope banned Orsini from seeing Lee and Lee herself was ordered to leave the country. A well-publicised joint suicide attempt only added to the furore surrounding the couple but the relationship, and ensuing scandal, had changed Lee. No longer a relatively obscure 'Rank starlet', she was now a major European celebrity. Her estranged husband Lucas duly demanded a divorce – and a settlement from the wealthy Orsini. Rank, furious that their painstakingly constructed image of Lee as a compliant blonde had been obliterated by her sexual adventures on the continent, promptly terminated her contract.

It wasn't long before Lee was reported to be losing interest in her career as an actress, despite by now being in demand with both German and Italian film-makers. She also lost interest in Prince Orsini and began a new romance with the controversial Italian film-maker Gualtiero Jacopetti, best known for *Mondo Cane* – the original 'shockumentary'.[15] In March 1961, while visiting California, twenty-five-year-old Lee, Jacopetti and his co-director Paolo Cavara were being driven from Las Vegas to Los Angeles when their driver lost control near San Bernardino after a rear tyre blew at more than one hundred miles an hour. The car flipped over catapulting Lee sixty-three feet from the front passenger seat into the surrounding desert where she died some twenty minutes later. Jacopetti, Cavara and the driver suffered only minor injuries. Fifteen people attended her funeral including Orsini. Her parents remained in London. Six months later, at Orsini's request, Lee's ashes were interred in the Protestant Cemetery in Rome, where Keats and Shelley are buried. When Jacopetti died fifty years later at the age of ninety-one, he asked to be buried next to her. Gossip columnist Dorothy Kilgallen reported that Lee's spectacular death had caused sadness but little surprise. Apparently people who knew her had a feeling she was 'building up to a big finish'. She was calm enough when married to her first husband but the 'recklessness took over' after she went to Italy and became involved with Prince Orsini.[16] (Just four years later, Killgallen built up to her own 'big finish' and died from an overdose of alcohol and barbiturates.)

By the time Lee had made her way to Italy to embrace all things Italian, the second of Kashfi's contemporaries, Anna Maria Pierangeli, had already left the country of her birth. She had made her way to Los Angeles where, in the space of six short years, her once promising career foundered and her off-screen life unravelled. Like Kashfi, Pierangeli found herself, at the age of twenty-five, living as a single parent in a place where nothing made sense. The two women also shared difficult relationships with their mothers, albeit employing different ways of dealing with them, and both turned to chemical solutions to help them cope with the colossal bewilderment their downfalls would eventually engender.

Pier Angeli was born in Sardinia under Mussolini's reign and grew up in Rome during World War Two, enduring

first the acute shortage of food, then the aerial bombard-
ment and then the German Occupation. The horrors she
witnessed during this period remained with her. Angeli
dreamt of being an architect like her father, Luigi
Pierangeli, to whom she was devoted and, like Kashfi
over a thousand miles away, she went to art school. And
like Kashfi, a random encounter with the film world – in
this case the directors Vittorio De Sica and Leonide Moguy
– changed the course of her life. De Sica, fresh from his
international success with *Bicycle Thieves*, appeared alongside Angeli in the film which would bring her to the
attention of the Hollywood director Fred Zinnemann and
jump-start her career in Hollywood. *Domani e troppo tardi*
(*Tomorrow is Too Late*) was directed by Moguy and fea-
tured an acclaimed performance by the inexperienced
Angeli. Before the film was released she had already been
offered the lead in an American film, *Teresa*. Screenwriter
Stewart Stern, who went on to write *Rebel Without a
Cause*, based the screenplay of *Teresa* in part upon his
own experiences during the war. He became a close friend
of Angeli's and when MGM came calling Stern had strong
advice for the family:

> When they came to see me, I pleaded with Signora
> Pierangeli to be careful. I said, 'I don't know if anything
> will happen after this picture but I do know that you must
> never live in Hollywood. I don't know if you can grow up
> normally in Rome, but you can't in Hollywood. It just
> won't work. If MGM wants to sign you for a longer time,
> you must make it clear in the contract that you will never
> live in Los Angeles. You can go there to work, but you

must keep your apartment in Rome.' Mrs Pierangeli agreed, and solemnly swore that that was what they would do.[17]

Angeli spent her eighteenth birthday in New York where she had arrived from Italy three days earlier to film her American scenes. At the Waldorf Astoria, with her mother, Stewart Stern and Arthur Loew, the president of MGM, Angeli went to the Starlight Room cabaret where Vic Damone, an Italian-American crooner following in Frank Sinatra's footsteps, sang 'Happy Birthday' to her. She also met Marlon Brando who visited Fred Zinnemann on location. Brando had made his first film *The Men* with Zinnemann – and would later reacquaint himself with Angeli. Before she returned to Italy, MGM decided that their new starlet's name, Anna Maria Pierangeli, was too long for the lights over a marquee and changed it. They split her surname in half and from then on her professional name was Pier Angeli, although she remained Anna to her family and friends. Angeli considered Pier a 'boy's name' and always hated it.

Soon after *Teresa* opened to widespread critical acclaim, Luigi Pierangeli died at the early age of forty-four. Life changed overnight for the family. Six years after suffering the privations of the war, Mrs Pierangeli, a widow with three young daughters and no income, faced a hard choice. Stay in Italy, as she had promised Stern, with family and friends, or make a new life in a strange country. She chose the new life and allowed MGM to take charge. A house was found in the Brentwood area of Los Angeles and nineteen-year-old Angeli supported her family on a salary of $1,600 a month, plus living expenses. As Stern later said, it was then that 'the whole baloney started'. Within a year MGM was making serious headway in building the petite, waif-like Angeli into a 'star of tomorrow'. She featured regularly on the covers of *Life*, *Paris-Match*, *Modern Screen* and *Photoplay* while competing for roles alongside MGM's other European import Leslie Caron. Caron was a year older than Angeli and possessed a similar, childlike appeal which served her well in roles like *Gigi*. Esme Chandlee, the studio publicist who would later befriend Kashfi, played a key role in supporting Angeli:

> I was assigned to Anna Angeli. She was innocent and very shy to start with. She was smart, but very emotional both on and off the screen. I think she'd been a Daddy's girl and I recognised a dependent personality – always wanting someone to look after her. What she needed was one big break.[18]

The first big break went to Caron rather than Angeli in the title role in *Lili* which went on to win four 'Oscars' including Best Actress for Caron. Although both Angeli and Caron projected similar young urchin-style images it was Angeli who was frequently pictured at home surrounded by her dolls, stuffed toys and the two dogs which had been given to her by the studio. MGM, despite casting her in romantic situations with older stars such as Kirk Douglas, continued to go to great lengths to maintain Angeli's noticeably childish appearance for as long as possible – even inserting clauses in her contract which forbade her to dye her hair, pluck her eyebrows or wear heavy make-up. This suited the overprotective Mrs Pierangeli, who struggled with what she regarded as the free and easy life of the American teenager and insisted on micro-managing every aspect of Angeli's life – including buying all her daughter's clothes. Even after Angeli married Vic Damone, her mother continued to manage her career.

Angeli's closest friend was Debbie Reynolds, another teenage contract player who had suddenly hit the big time following the huge success of *Singin' in the Rain*. She also spent time with the Italian starlet, Anna Maria Alberghetti, who would later take Kashfi's place in *Ten Thousand Bedrooms*. Brando was another frequent visitor to the Angeli household and was much admired by Mrs Pierangeli who regarded him as 'the adorable son I never had, full of love, sensibility and great compassion...'[19]

In an indication of the central role which MGM played in Angeli's life, Eddie Mannix, the general manager of MGM, played surrogate father and walked her down the aisle at her wedding to Vic Damone in November 1954. Mannix worked alongside Howard Strickling and between them they guarded their assets closely. Prior to marrying Damone, Angeli had passionate (and highly publicised) relationships with both Kirk Douglas and James Dean. Mrs Pierangeli disapproved strongly of her daughter's choice of men and was instrumental in ensuring that Angeli broke up with them. The Italian crooner, Vic Damone, by contrast was thought to be a safer bet – and he was known to the family because he had previously dated Angeli's twin sister, Marisa Pavan. In fact the couple barely knew each other. They had met again by chance and married less than two months later in November 1955 in an elaborate studio-organised publicity extravaganza.

Angeli's pregnancy was announced soon after and Perry, named after his godfather, the singer Perry Como, was born almost nine months later. The first photographs of the baby, complete with ecstatic parents, were released the week that James Dean died in September 1955 – the date that coincided with Kashfi's arrival in America. Angeli, according to her mother, was 'tormented forever' by the untimely and shocking death of her former lover.[20]

A month later, Angeli left her baby and her husband and headed to London to make *Port Afrique*, her first film in nearly two years. This was the pattern of their disastrous, and short-lived, marriage. Damone travelled from coast to coast singing for a living while Angeli went wherever the studio sent her. The new parents spent a lot of time apart both from their child, who was looked after by a German governess, and each other. Damone disliked his wife's career as an actress and, in particular, her proximity to her leading men, and gave frequent interviews to the press where he expressed his desire for Angeli to abandon her career and stay at home with the baby. The relationship was volatile, with rumours of Damone's violent behaviour towards Angeli contrasting sharply with the studio-driven publicity shots of the 'happy couple'. Two years after marrying Damone, Angeli, apparently under pressure from her husband, broke her contract with MGM. She was twenty-five years old. Her mother, who was still being paid by the studio to manage her daughter's career, suddenly found herself without an income. Despite this, publicist Esme Chandlee held Mrs Pierangeli responsible for Angeli's decision to walk away from the studio:

> She had pushed and pushed her daughter, and truly, she had Anna's best interests at heart, but Enrica (Mrs Pierangeli) thought Anna was a star when she was still a starlet.

MGM agreed with Chandlee. According to Angeli's biographer, Jane Allen:

> Pier was still a starlet in the eyes of the studio bosses – she had never been anything more – and they let her go without protest. But the system made certain she couldn't find work in Hollywood.

Angeli herself would simply say later, 'It was a catastrophe – the beginning of the end.'[21]

Kashfi and Angeli met through their mutual MGM publicist Esme Chandlee and soon became close friends. Kashfi remembered that, 'she showed me girl stuff, where to shop, where to get my dresses made... when I became pregnant she gave me a beautiful baby shower and when I went into labour she called her own doctor.' Angeli, for her part, told a journalist that she and Kashfi were 'like sisters.'[22] Indeed, Kashfi maintained in her autobiography that while she was pregnant and Brando had moved out, Angeli 'monitored my safety by telephone several times each day'.[23] Chandlee, having got them together, came to believe that Kashfi provided the 'wrong sort of model of a deserted wife for Pier, even unconsciously, to follow.'[24]

Angeli did indeed first consult a lawyer regarding a divorce from Damone during May 1958 when Kashfi was estranged from Brando and awaiting the birth of her son. She then formally separated from him at the end of August while Kashfi left Brando the following month: two young women cutting themselves adrift from relationships they believed to be intolerable at the same time. They were also, for the first time since they had embarked upon their lives in Los Angeles, without the protection and stability of the studio – which, for all its faults, provided an income, a shield from the insatiably salacious press, a measure of a structure in their lives and the opportunity to work. Without these things, that protection, they were in freefall. While Kashfi chose to remain in California, her career effectively over, Angeli drifted around Europe with her young son in tow picking up work wherever she could find it. Her best role was as Richard Attenborough's wife in *The Angry Silence* which she filmed in London in 1960: it won BAFTA's and much critical acclaim, yet it led nowhere. She returned to Italy, changed her name back to Anna Maria Pierangeli and embarked upon a second, even more calamitous, marriage. She was to make another fifteen films over the remaining decade of her life including *Love Me, Love My Wife*, an X-rated, mildly pornographic movie filmed under the title *Addio Alexandra* in Holland and Rome. Angeli accepted the role believing it would never be shown in the United States but, to her great embarrassment, it was not only screened but also reviewed in both *Variety* and the *Hollywood Reporter* during the final months of her life. Most upsetting for her was the *Hollywood Reporter's* comment 'Perhaps the unhappiest element is the appearance of Pier Angeli.'[25] But possibly her professional nadir was her final film, *Octaman,* about a murderous monster octopus – it is hard to imagine anything further from her poignant performance as Paul Newman's wife in the Oscar-winning *Somebody Up There Likes Me* fifteen years earlier.

As Angeli struggled to pay her bills, she became, like Blanche Dubois, utterly dependent on the kindness of strangers – yet found few of them. Her life disintegrated around her as she drifted from one more or less abusive relationship to the next. Having run out of options in Europe she returned to Los Angeles and stayed with her former acting coach, Helena Sorrel, in her one-bedroom apartment. Sorrel, aware that Angeli was mixing an unknown quantity of prescription drugs with copious amounts of alcohol, found the situation 'sheer hell' and thought that Angeli was 'deranged'.[26] It didn't last long. Eight months after her return to Los Angeles, Pier Angeli died from an apparently accidental overdose of barbiturates at the age of thirty-nine.

Gia Scala is the final player in Kashfi's circle of fellow starlets. Peter Manso, Brando's biographer, maintains that Brando dated both Angeli and Gia Scala in the 1950s. Scala's sister, Tina, disagrees, believing that, at the time, she was grieving for the death of her mother. Whatever the truth of it, she had more than Brando in common with Angeli. Scala's father was Italian and her mother Irish and, although born in Liverpool, she moved to Sicily as a baby. Like Angeli, her childhood was disfigured by war. When Scala was nine years old, in 1943, Sicily became the base for the invasion of Italy by the Allied forces – as well as a training ground for many of the men who, eleven months later, would land on the beaches of Normandy.

Five years later, the fourteen-year-old Scala moved to America to live with her Irish Aunt Agata in Long Island. She was spotted by a Universal Studios executive while appearing as a contestant on a quiz show on television and invited to Los Angeles to screen test for the role of Mary Magdalene. The prospective film, *The Galileans*, was never produced but Scala made the most of her lucky break. Universal Studios put her through the usual makeover process; dying her hair dark brown, capping her teeth and changing her name from Josephine (or Giovanna) Scoglio to Gia Scala. Her own name, like Pier Angeli's, was considered too long for a marquee. After trying Scala out in an uncredited non-speaking role in *All That Heaven Allows* (starring Rock Hudson), Universal placed her in their famous 'star school'.[27] She was offered a salary of $100 a week – a decent wage in 1955. Decent enough for Scala and her mother to rent in the Villa Sands apartment block next door to Clint Eastwood. He was also a $100 weekly contract player with Universal – for a short time. After a series of uncredited roles Eastwood was dropped by the studio in October 1955. Three years later the new medium of television rescued him when *Rawhide* came along. Scala had better luck with Universal. She made a total of fifteen films during her six-year career – including Kashfi's near miss, *Don't Go Near The Water*. Replacing Kashfi in the film led to a lifelong friendship between the two women. Scala also knew Angeli. There is a photograph of them together seated at a table at Angeli's baby shower in the summer of 1955. Scala, newly arrived in Los Angeles, wears a glamorous-looking dress (the same one she would wear on her wedding day four years later) while a heavily pregnant Angeli has a champagne glass in front of her.[28]

Unlike Kashfi, Scala had a close relationship with her mother and Mrs Scoglio's death in 1957, just as Scala's career was gathering momentum, derailed her. Her behaviour became erratic; while filming in London she tried to jump off Waterloo Bridge. Back in America, she was booked for driving while drunk in Los Angeles and then burst into tears during a live television interview while promoting *Don't Go Near The Water*. Despite Scala's explanation that she was distressed following her mother's recent illness and death, she began to be seen as unstable. In Basinger's terminology that meant she was turning into a 'nasty surprise' – someone who might jeopardise the studio's financial investment in them and therefore needed to be 'rooted out'.[29] According to Scala's sister, Tina, her publicist and friend Dore Freeman was concerned about the negative press she was getting and suggested a solution:

He recognised that Gia was distraught from Mother's passing. She was alone in Hollywood, no family for support. Dore thought the best solution for her was to marry.[30]

In August 1959, Scala duly married the actor Don Burnett, a close friend of Rock Hudson's. Freeman, apparently, thought they would be compatible as they both shared a passion for art; they certainly made a handsome couple, tall, athletic-looking and sociable – and both were on track to become major stars. Once again the speedy marriage was troubled from the start and just over a year after the wedding they separated, temporarily. Burnett, like Vic Damone, disliked the fact that his wife's job meant she was often away from home and so to save her marriage Scala agreed to give up her career. There was one final film role – opposite Gregory Peck in *The Guns of Navarone* in 1961 – for which she was paid $100,000. She then obediently complied with Burnett's demand and, apart from occasional television appearances, didn't work again. Instead Scala's time was spent playing tennis, entertaining Burnett's new business acquaintances (he had switched careers and was now an investment banker) – and drinking. Eight years later, Burnett left Scala and moved in with Rock Hudson.[31] He later married another actress, Barbara Anderson, who was fifteen years younger than him. Anderson, who was making a name for herself in television shows like *Ironside*, also gave up her career to be married to Burnett.

Scala was now thirty-five; an ex-actress without a job and she quickly fell apart. She was repeatedly arrested for drink-driving, and also for harassing her now ex-husband. Suffering from depression, she made several suicide attempts overdosing on ketamine and on cockroach poison.[32] At one point, after Scala had been detained in a psychiatric hospital, Kashfi applied to have her discharged into her care and Scala lived with her and her now teenaged son Christian for a couple of months.[33] Less than a year later, in April 1972, Scala died in her apart-

ment at the age of thirty-eight – reportedly from an accidental overdose of drugs and alcohol. Scala's death hit
Kashfi hard, happening in the midst of the most shocking
drama of her custody battles with Brando – the kidnapping
of her son. She later wrote that it 'brought to me, with a
shock, the realization of my mortality'.[34]

Scala's death followed six months after Angeli's. Kashfi
and Angeli had shared long years of bitter court battles
with their ex-husbands, often in front of the same judges,
with allegations of verbal abuse and physical intimidation
– and, most painfully, estrangement from their sons.
Kashfi remained preoccupied after the loss of her close
ally and said; 'Her spindly figure, wistful face, and deli-
cate, winning smile haunted my thoughts, much as I
feared dwelling on the similarities of our lives'.[35]

What do the lonely, unlovely and unbearable deaths of
Angeli and Scala tell us? That it's hard to survive in an
unforgiving world. That some people are more fragile than
others. That some events, like useless husbands, abusive
relationships or the deaths of people close to you, are
simply not survivable for everyone. And, of course, when
your dreams slip beneath the surface and then your head
does as well, perhaps you too become unbearable and
unlovely. In a landscape where alcohol and prescription
drugs are readily available, it's easy to succumb. *Valley of
the Dolls* may have been pulp fiction but it was also
prophetic – at least for Scala and Angeli. They did indeed
become *too* battered and *too* weary to enjoy anything. No
wonder Jacqueline Susann would not entertain the idea
of a 'fucking happy ending'.[36] And what of Lee? Unlike

Angeli or Scala there is not a significant film performance on which to judge her talent – but there is at least, perhaps, a glimpse of bravado and the sense that she believed in herself.

Meanwhile Kashfi, despite being blown in the same unforgiving direction as Lee, Angeli and Scala, abandoned by husband and studio, and seemingly destined to self-destruction, nevertheless – almost miraculously – outlived friends, husbands, and her own child.

Notes

[1] Jacqueline Susann, *Valley of the Dolls*, (Virago Press, 2004), prelim pages.

[2] Ibid.

[3] Barbara Seaman, *Lovely Me: The Life of Jacqueline Susann*, (Seven Stories Press, 1996), p. 298.

[4] Martin Chilton, 'Valley of the Dolls: from reject to 30-million bestseller', *The Telegraph*, 8 May 2016.

[5] Barbara Seaman, *Lovely Me: The Life of Jacqueline Susann*, p. 314.

[6] Kirk Crivello, *Fallen Angels: The Lives and Untimely Deaths of Fourteen Hollywood Beauties*, (Futurs, 1991), p. 90.

[7] Julie Burchill, Introduction, *Valley of the Dolls*, (Virago Press, 2004), p. x.

[8] George Englund, *The Naked Brando: Portrait of a Friendship*, (Gibson Square, 2010), p. 44.

[9] Barbara Seaman, *Lovely Me: The Life of Jacqueline Susann*, p. 290.

[10] Matthew Sweet , *Shepperton Babylon: The Lost Worlds of British Cinema*, (Faber and Faber, 2006), p. 231.

[11] Annette Kuhn, *The Women's Companion to International Film*, (University of California, 1994), p. 47.

[12] Amanda Mason, 'What Were The Baedeker Raids?' Imperial War Museum.

[13] Richard Koper, *Fifties Blondes: Sexbombs, Sirens, Bad Girls and Teen Queens* (BearManor Media, 2015), Loc 1333, Kindle ed.

[14] http://www.glamourgirlsofthesilverscreen.com

[15] *The Independent*, 31 August 2011.

[16] http://www.glamourgirlsofthesilverscreen.com

[17] Jane Allen, *Pier Angeli: A Fragile Life*, (McFarland & Company, 2002), Chapter Three 'Teresa', Kindle ed.

[18] Ibid.

[19] Ibid., Chapter Eight 'Perry', Kindle ed.

[20] Ibid.

[21] Ibid., Chapter Nine 'The Bubble Bursts', Kindle ed.

[22] Ibid.

[23] Anna Kashfi & E.P. Stein, *Brando's Bride*, (Crown Publishers, 1979), p. 116.

[24] Jane Allen, *Pier Angeli: A Fragile Life*, Chapter Nine 'The Bubble Bursts', Kindle ed.

[25] *Hollywood Reporter*, 8 June 1971.

[26] Jane Allen, *Pier Angeli: A Fragile Life*, Chapter Nine 'The Bubble Bursts', Kindle ed.

[27] Jeanine Basinger, *The Star Machine*, (Vintage Books, 2009), p. 523.

[28] Sterling Saint James, *Gia Scala: The First Gia*, (Parhelion House, 2015), p. 190.

[29] Jeanine Basinger, *The Star Machine*, p. 38.

[30] Sterling Saint James, *Gia Scala: The First Gia*, p. 282.

[31] Ibid., p. 320.

[32] Kirk Crivello, *Fallen Angels: The Lives and Untimely Deaths of Fourteen Hollywood Beauties,* p. 216.

[33] Ibid.

[34] Anna Kashfi, *Brando for Breakfast*, p. 241.

[35] Ibid.

[36] Barbara Seaman, *Lovely Me: The Life of Jacqueline Susann*, pp. 298-299.

11

Dirty Drugs

More than a medical phenomenon, the little white pill shaped an era. For millions of Americans, Miltown was a new and seemingly harmless drug to be experienced, experimented with, and enjoyed.[1]

Andrea Tone, The Age of Anxiety:
A History of America's Turbulent Affair with Tranquilizers

Bruised, barefoot and belligerent, actress Anna Kashfi, 30, bailed out of jail today after allegedly slugging a police officer in a 24-hour bout of violence with her ex-husband Marlon Brando, over custody of their six-year-old son.[2]

Los Angeles Herald-Examiner, December 8th 1964

A couple of weeks before Marlon Brando married Anna Kashfi he gave her half a Miltown. To be fair, she had just told him that her father had been murdered in New Delhi and he probably thought that the new wonder drug would help calm her down. For Kashfi it was 'the first time in my life I resorted to a pill for consolation'.[3] Unfortunately, mostly for her, it wouldn't be the last.

Prescription drugs were not a new phenomenon but the arrival of Miltown was truly revolutionary. Its spectacular and unexpected success normalised anxiety.[4] Now for the first time, as Andrea Tone, author of *The Age of*

Anxiety, noted, it was permissible to see doctors in search of something to make you feel better about the vagaries of life, not just to treat diseases. Miltown paved the way for Valium in the 1970s and Prozac in the 1990s. It opened the door to an era of lifestyle drugs by rendering anxiety accessible to scientific scrutiny. Within a year of its arrival, a staggering one in twenty Americans had tried it – including Marlon Brando who, according to his assistant Alice Marchak, 'was never without it'.[5]

Miltown, 'psychiatry's first mass-market blockbuster' drug, was developed by a Czech refugee working in a public health laboratory in Yorkshire during World War Two.[6] Frank Berger was a microbiologist, one of hundreds of scientists in Britain and the United States working on how to produce penicillin in the quantities in which it was needed. He realised that the mephenesin (a chemically-modified version of a disinfectant) he was experimenting with as a penicillin preservative had a relaxing effect when he injected it into mice. By 1947, Berger's 'mouse-relaxer' was being used on humans but there were downsides; it only lasted for a few hours, it had a greater effect on the spinal cord than the brain and it was less potent in oral form.[7] After the war, having lost his parents and friends in the concentration camps, Berger moved to the United States to start a new life. While living in New Jersey and working at the Wallace Laboratories, Berger developed meprobamate, a tranquillizing compound which resolved the shortcomings of the 'mouse-relaxer'. It also offered an alternative to barbiturates, which sedated rather than calmed. He called the drug Miltown after a nearby village, Milltown (Wallace Laboratories had a habit of coding their compounds by the names of nearby towns). Berger also had a classification for his new drug; it was a tranquillizer, although he had originally wanted to call it a sedative.

Miltown was launched on May 9th 1955, but it took a time for what became known as Miltown mania to kick in. For the first couple of months the drug sold slowly but by August sales started to increase and by Christmas they exceeded $2 million.[8] The manufacturers, Carter Products, were puzzled by the rapid rise in sales until they realised that a particular community had taken to the drug. The entertainment industry, who felt itself to be routinely stressed and under a lot of pressure, had noticed the soothing properties of Miltown. And because this was an era, according to Andrea Tone, before the use of prescription drugs became stigmatised, celebrities publicly endorsed the wonders of the little white pill. Television host Milton Berle, whose weekly variety show was watched by millions of Americans, and intellectuals including Tennessee Williams and Aldous Huxley discussed the benefits of using the drug in interviews. In fact, Milton Berle was *such* a fan of the drug and *so* keen to tell his audience how good it made him feel that he began to call himself 'Uncle Miltown'. The enormous amount of publicity, as well as the endorsement of the drug by some of the most glamorous and influential people in America, resulted in a consumer frenzy across the country. Los Angeles, home to many rich and famous people, was the drug's first major marketplace and was referred to as 'Miltown-by-the-sea'.[9] Schwabs on Sunset Boulevard (known as 'The Drugstore of the Stars') also delivered direct to the home – and Brando was just one star who received a weekly parcel of drugs.[10] As Miltown mania kicked off during the winter of 1955-56, Schwabs sold a staggering 250,000 of the 'don't-give-a-damn pills'.[11] There were, of course, ways of obtaining the drug which didn't involve doctors or pharmacies – from private parties to bars selling alcoholic blends such as the 'Guided Missile' (a double shot of vodka plus two Miltowns) and the perennially popular 'Miltini' (a dry martini with a pill replacing the olive).[12] In short, more or less anyone who wanted to pop the pill could. It was the right drug at the right time:

> This was a period, after the war, the 1950s, when Americans were working hard and felt entitled to something that could get them through the day and what was so attractive about this drug was, many people taking it did not think they had anything seriously wrong and did not refer to themselves as psychiatric patients. For many it was emotional aspirin, a peace pill.[13]

By 1956 Miltown's popularity had spread throughout the nation and, for some, became part of their daily life. A decade later, when John Cheever's short story 'The Swimmer' was being filmed with Burt Lancaster as Neddy Merrill, Cheever visited the set near his home in Ossining, in Westchester County, New York. To fortify himself he drank a pint of whisky, some martinis, a few glasses of wine topped off with 'a Miltown for good measure.'[14]

As for Frank Berger, he was intrigued by *why* people had become dependent on Miltowns to get them through the day:

These people are not insane; they simply are over excitable and irritable, and create crisis situations over things that are unimportant. What is the physiological basis of this over excitability?[15]

Berger wasn't just referring to members of the film community in this statement – but he might have been. In a profession where every fault is magnified, every inch of your life crawled over by gossip columnists and you are, sometimes, working the kind of hours that would drive a sane person insane – perhaps overexcitability and irritability isn't so unfathomable.

Hollywood itself was no stranger to drugs. Stories abound of fatal addiction, from Barbara 'too beautiful for Hollywood' La Marr's cocaine cravings in the 1920s to Judy Garland's infamous amphetamine habit in the 1950s.[16] What distinguishes these women's stories is that the drugs were prescribed by the studio doctors for industrial purposes. La Marr, 'MGM's first official publicity problem', was supplied with cocaine and morphine so that she could keep on working when she had sprained her ankle during a dance routine in the aptly titled film *Souls for Sale* in 1923.[17] Three years later, at the age of twenty-nine, she achieved lasting notoriety as one of the first drug-related deaths in the film community. The studio publicity machine blamed La Marr's untimely demise on 'vigorous dieting'.[18] 'Vigorous dieting' also played a significant role in the studio's handling of Judy Garland's chronic drug addiction. While still a teenager, she was prescribed a combination of Benzedrine, Phenobarbital, Seconal and the newly-available amphetamines alongside a diet of soup and cottage cheese to keep her weight under control and her energetic enough to work fifteen-hour shifts. After thirty-four years as an addict, Garland died in the bathroom of a rented house in London. The coroner listed her cause of her death as 'an incautious self-overdosage of barbiturates'.[19] The equivalent of ten capsules of Seconal was found in her blood, but not in her stomach; in other words, she had enough drugs roaming around her system at all times to kill her at any time.

Phenobarbital was developed in 1912 as a treatment for epileptic seizures and is still used today. In the 1930s and 1940s, when Garland first started taking it, it was also widely prescribed for a variety of ailments including anxiety (it was before Miltown came on the market). As there is no mention of Garland suffering from epilepsy she was probably prescribed it as a tranquiliser. Both Phenobarbital and Seconal are sedatives. Garland, in order to survive her punishing work schedule, had somehow to simultaneously stave off fatigue *and* combat the drowsiness caused by the sedatives.

Benzedrine, amphetamine's first incarnation, launched in 1932, was the drug that did the waking-up part of the job. Originally introduced as an inhaler for for nasal congestion it was soon, like Miltown, regarded as a 'wonder-drug' and prescribed for a range of conditions.[20] During World War Two, it was widely distributed amongst front-line troops by German, American and British military authorities. 'Back home bennies', as the pills were called, became enormously popular both as an appetite suppressant and for their dramatic ability to decrease sleepiness.

Poets, pop-stars and politicians were amongst those who became addicted. W. H. Auden began each day with bennies and ended it with alcohol and barbiturates.[21] Elvis Presley started using them in the early 1950s to overcome his shyness. Around the same time, Anthony Eden, the British politician, began taking them to offset problems caused by a botched gallstones operation. By 1955, when Eden succeeded Winston Churchill as Prime Minister, he was using Benzedrine to boost his confidence apparently unaware that, over time, amphetamine users acquire tolerance and therefore have to increase their dose to continue to achieve the required effect. The following year, during the Suez Crisis Eden confessed that he was 'practically living on Benzedrine'.[22] According to Leslie Iverson in *The Science of Amphetamines*, Eden's 'paranoid personal animosity towards Colonel Nasser showed all the hallmarks of a man in the grip of amphetamines'. Suez was a catastrophe for Eden and his chronic lack of judgement destroyed his reputation. Along with his Benzedrine addiction, he was also taking Drinamyl, a combined amphetamine and barbiturate nicknamed Purple Hearts, for his abdominal pain. Drinamyl was banned in 1978.

In the summer of 1958, while trying to cope with a new baby and an indifferent husband, Kashfi:

> First teetered onto the alphabetized descent into oblivion – alcohol...barbiturates...that opened before me. I had known of Hollywood figures, several of them personal acquaintances, who followed such a trajectory to its lethal conclusion. Drinking, moderate at first, becomes an

179

automatic resource for dulling emotional pain. Red jackets, yellow jackets (Seconal, Nembutal), and others in the sorority of dolls (as Jacqueline Susann called them) lift the anxieties of insecurity and paint a fuzzy glow over the sharp edges of daily conflicts.[23]

The reference to *alphabetized descent* is interesting. She doesn't specify whether cocaine and LSD (which Cary Grant, Esther Williams – AKA 'Hollywood's Mermaid' – and Judy Balaban, wife of Brando's agent Jay Kanter, were fans of at the time) were also on the list but Phenobarbital definitely was.[24] Whatever combination of prescription drugs Kashfi was taking alongside her conspicuous alcohol consumption they led to her teetering, and finally toppling, headlong into an abyss in which she lost not her life, but her child – and any shred of anything she could call an existence. It was a long and inelegant stumble to the bottom with the fall measured, bleakly, in court appearances and newspaper headlines.

In 1959 there were two significant news stories concerning Kashfi – but no mention yet of anything badly awry. The first concerned the details of the Brandos' divorce in April. The *Daily Mirror* led with, 'Mrs. Brando Gets Divorce and £200,000 from Marlon'.[25] In a decade when more than seventy per cent of British workers were in manual labour and earning an average weekly wage of around £14, and just over a million women were secretaries or typists, £200,000 would have been a staggering amount of money. The *Mirror* was quick to tot up the amounts that 'dark skinned actress Anna Kashfi' would receive:

Today's settlement means that Miss Kashfi gets about £18,000 at once. She also gets custody of her son, Christian Devi, aged one. Brando, 35, will pay an extra £350 a month for the boy's support. And if Miss Kashfi is still unmarried at the end of ten years, it has been agreed that she can ask Brando for MORE cash on top of the £200,000 which he will have paid by then.

The second news story involving Kashfi that year was a *Daily Mirror* front page confession, apparently: 'Anna: Yes, I *am* from Cardiff'. For the previous two years, following the furore after her wedding, Kashfi maintained that her parents were an unmarried Indian couple called Selma Ghose and Devi Kashfi and not William and Phoebe O'Callaghan. In December the *Mirror* splashed the following:

> Many statements have been attributed to me, some falsely. If any of these have caused distress to Mr and Mrs O'Callaghan, it is a matter of regret to me. I do not wish to repudiate their claim with regard to my parenthood. Since it is clear that they wish to see me, I will see them at some time when we can meet in decent privacy. My years of childhood and youth are a closed book and must remain so.[26]

Kashfi's sudden decision to tell a different version of her story stemmed from the unforeseen newspaper stunt which the *Daily Express* staged when she returned Britain for the first time since she had left to pursue a career as an actress. Kashfi had arrived in the country with her

18-month-old son, perhaps to test the water and see whether she could settle there or perhaps just to meet her agent and make plans for work. Whatever the reason, the press lost no time in haranguing her for not meeting up with her parents. Days of disapproving headlines concerned Kashfi's neglect of (as the *Daily Express* called them) 'the old folks':

A Surprise For Her Mum Anna (Plus Baby) Flies In – But Not To See the Old Folks[27]

The paper made it clear that Kashfi would not be going to Cardiff and the 'old folks' wouldn't be coming to London. An unhappy-sounding Phoebe O'Callaghan was reported as saying, 'I shan't be going to see her in London, not after what she has done to me'.[28] Despite the entrenched positions taken by mother and daughter, the newspaper decided to intervene to try and force a reconciliation. They arranged for the O'Callaghans to take the train from Cardiff to London and arrive, unannounced, at the five-star Dorchester Hotel on Park Lane, where Kashfi was staying. In a cynical attempt to cause maximum embarrassment all round they then set up an impromptu press conference in the hotel lobby. Their efforts to stage a confrontation between the bewildered parents, who had never understood why Kashfi had disowned them, and their erstwhile daughter, who would never forgive the couple for their denial of her Indian ancestry, backfired when Kashfi refused to see them. The next day Sunday tabloid the *Empire News* (which would merge with the *News of the World* the following year) increased the pressure with a mawkish front-page plea to the uncompliant Kashfi. Written by Gareth Bowen who referred to himself as 'your old teenage friend', 'Come home Anna Kashfi!' admonished the actress to:

GO HOME FOR CHRISTMAS WITH YOUR BABY CHRISTIAN Your mother Anna? She needs you... heaven knows she needs you. Most of the day she weeps... and her hands haven't stopped trembling since you arrived in London. Every time there is a knock at the door the colour drains from her cheeks... always she hopes it's you and your baby – her grandson. It is Christmas, Anna... or shall I call you 'Joanna' as your parents do? You must go home...[29]

Faced with this onslaught Kashfi's agents Eric and Blanche Glass, who had steered her through her first film role in *The Mountain*, issued Kashfi's statement on the Tuesday and followed it with an apology, of sorts:

The O'Callaghans travelled from their Cardiff home Saturday to see Anna shortly after her arrival in London. The actress was not in and Monday night she apologised for their wasted journey. She agreed to see them 'at some time when we can meet in decent privacy'.[30]

Ignoring the heartfelt plea from her 'old teenage friend' Kashfi abruptly flew back to America 'to deal with urgent legal affairs' thereby avoiding any possible chance of 'decent privacy' time with her parents.[31] The meeting never did take place. Five years later Phoebe O'Callaghan died at home at the age of fifty-seven. As for Kashfi's 'years of childhood and youth remaining a closed book', so they did until 1979 when, in her autobiography *Brando for Breakfast*, she inexplicably repudiated her parents claim all over again.

Despite their intense interest in Kashfi's new-found wealth and parentage issues, the newspapers had not yet picked up on the turbulent post-divorce relationship between Brando and his ex-wife. According to Kashfi, the first violent altercation between the couple took place just two weeks after the settlement was agreed. Following that, there was a ceasefire of sorts while Brando spent weekdays in Milltown, the town his drug of choice was named after, filming *The Fugitive Kind* and his weekends in Los Angeles editing *One-Eyed Jacks*. Kashfi was relieved: 'For these few restful months I had no direct contact with Marlon. I was able to regain a measure of equilibrium, to bolster myself against the seduction of drugs and alcohol'.[32] It didn't last. By August 1960, they were regularly engaged in the open warfare which would carry on for more than a decade. The details of one incident, relayed in courtrooms, were ugly and unpleasant:

According to Marlon, she burst into his house one night while he was sleeping and hurled herself into his bed. When he told her to behave, she responded violently by slapping and biting him. Then, after he finally succeeded in ejecting Anna from the house, she tried to beat her way back in.When she broke through a window, Marlon seized her, threw her onto the bed, and tied her down with a sash from his robe. He summoned the police to have her taken off.[33]

Kashfi later admitted that she didn't entirely recall the events of that evening although she did remember the policeman who drove her home. She dismissed the rest as 'Marlon's usual hyperbole'.[34] Yet altercations like this became a routine cat and mouse game between them. Brando regularly objected to what he saw as Kashfi's interference with his visitation rights to their son while Kashfi's stream of counter-accusations included the allegations that he hired detectives to follow and harass her, that he frequently hit her and that his morals were questionable. Back and forth they went every few months, while Brando continued to make films (including the epic *Mutiny on the Bounty*), marry other women, and father other children.

By the summer of 1963 Kashfi was being prescribed Dilantin for epilepsy alongside other drugs. Dilantin was the commercial name for Phenytoin which, as well as being used as an anti-seizure drug, was also prescribed to control nervousness and depression. The side effects included an altered mental state, confusion and loss of memory. Kashfi was mixing Dilantin with barbiturates – most likely Nembutal, Seconal or Amytal as these three were the most widely prescribed at that time – and excessive amounts of alcohol. It was a potentially lethal combination. Robert Walker, the actor who starred alongside Judy Garland in her first non-singing role in *The Clock*, died at the age of thirty-two from the effects of combining alcohol and Amytal in 1952.[35] Over the years, whenever Brando challenged his ex-wife's ability to look after Christian, he repeatedly referred to Kashfi's barbiturate consumption – and to the fact that she was drunk.

In December 1964, five months after the death of her mother and seven years after taking her first Miltown, Kashfi's chemical gamble finally caught up with her – with catastrophic consequences. Once again, she had only a 'hazy' memory of what happened.[36] Brando on the other hand, according to his testimony at the custody hearing three months later, had perfect recall. The ruinous events involved a gun, barbiturates, members of the Los Angeles Police Force, Brando, his lawyers, his private detectives and his assistant, hotel staff – and a six-year-old boy. 'Brando's Ex Jailed For Socking Police' was the following day's front-page headline in the *Los Angeles Herald-Examiner*, an evening paper with the largest circulation in America, complete with a picture of a dishevelled, sullen-looking Kashfi in her dressing gown sitting half in and half out of the door of a car with one bare, elegant foot pointing down, ballerina-style, towards the road.[37] The caption read 'Midnight Battle Over Son' and detailed the escalation of her behaviour from private fury at Brando to public frustration with the police. After overdosing on what was later described by Brando as '4 mgs of a short-acting barbiturate, a very dangerous dosage' (whether accidentally or deliberately is disputed), Kashfi ended up in the emergency ward at her local hospital.[38] Her son, who had called the police department when he couldn't rouse her, was collected by his father. The next morning Kashfi discharged herself from hospital and went looking for Christian. After breaking down a fence she walked into her ex-husband's house and, according to Brando 'created a window-smashing, secretary-slapping scene'.[39] This involved punching Alice Marchak who was looking after Christian while Brando was at work and throwing a table through a plate glass window before she then 'ran off with our child'. Brando by now aware, apparently for the first time, that Kashfi kept a loaded revolver at her home which she messed about with when drunk, believed his son to be in 'extreme and immediate danger'.[40] He obtained a court order and headed off to find them. Meanwhile, in anticipation of Brando's pursuit, Kashfi had left her home and checked into the Bel-Air Sands Hotel on Sunset Boulevard under an alias and, as she later recalled, 'acted as inconspicuously as my turbulent state of mind had permitted'.[41] The Bel-Air Sands hotel was a popular haunt of Hollywood's finest; Marilyn Monroe, Montgomery Clift and Tony Curtis all lived there during the 1950s. Coincidentally, Tarita Teriipaia, Brando's third wife (and his co-star in *Mutiny on the Bounty*) was also staying there that night. Brando was tipped off about Kashfi and Christian's arrival and arrived within the hour:

> Marlon, who was armed with a special emergency court order to assume custody, charged the lobby accompanied by Sergeant Ed Hall of the LAPD, attorney Allen Sussman, and two private detectives. A ferocious fight ensued with Anna. With her long black hair streaming over a pink nightgown and bathrobe, Anna attacked hotel manager Sterling Peck, desk clerk Beverley Ross, and hotel detective James Briscoe. She was arrested on the spot.[42]

Kashfi's version had it that she was in the bedroom of her suite getting ready for bed when she heard a commotion and went into the hallway to find Brando and several police officers 'dragging' Christian down the corridor. After racing after her son and confronting the police officers, she was handcuffed and taken to the nearest police station. She was charged with three counts of 'battery and disturbing the peace' before being released on $276 bail.[43] Undeterred by the charges, Kashfi immediately petitioned to reclaim her son alleging that Brando was living with Tarita Teriipaia out of wedlock – which made it an unsuitable household for her child.

In February 1965, at the fourteenth custody hearing since their divorce, Kashfi tried to explain her actions: 'On December 7th I did something stupid. I tried to kill myself but had enough sense not to take too many pills and told my son to call the operator for help'.[44] She admitted having the gun, 'a 22-caliber Beretta' because, she said, her life had been threatened. Brando then gave his side of the story:

> Soon after the baby was born, she began having fits and soon after that she began taking tranquilizers and barbiturates… from the time the child was three months old, visitation rights have been denied me periodically… Many times when I attempted to see the youngster, Miss Kashfi was in a drunken stupor. On one occasion she attempted to stab me; this occurred in front of the boy. On several other occasions, she threatened to kill me, the child and herself.[45]

Kashfi's character witness was a doctor who, after discussing her history of epileptic seizures, ventured this opinion of her behaviour:

Miss Kashfi has a wide, swinging personality, episodes of deep depression to normal elation, all with hysterical overtones... She was often in a moderately controlled hysterical state, sometimes appearing 'like a drunk.' Even as little a stimulus as a glass of beer could produce a reaction.[46]

After hearing the evidence, the judge decided that 'Miss Kashfi's reliance on drugs and alcohol both contributed to her uncontrollable temper' and ordered her to undergo a six-month rehabilitation programme.[47] He awarded custody of Christian to Brando but, in order to avoid the boy witnessing any more scenes between his parents, he also insisted that he live with one of Brando's sisters (Franny) and her husband on their farm in Illinois for six months.

Five months later, Kashfi went on trial for assault and battery. Brando testified that she was suffering from 'psychoneuroses, which at times caused hysterical blindness [...] barbiturate poisoning [...] occasional malnutrition [...] a psychological and physical addiction to barbiturates, alcohol, and tuberculosis'.[48] Kashfi was found guilty and sentenced to thirty days in jail or a fine of $200. She paid the fine. In October the pendulum swung back again:

Actress Wins Custody Case

The long, bitter struggle between actor Marlon Brando and actress Anna Kashfi over custody of their young son has taken another turn with Miss Kashfi this time winning custody. In awarding custody of Christian Devi, 7, to the

30 year old actress, Superior Court Judge A. A. Scott said yesterday: 'If this lady is left to lead her own life with her own son and without fights and obnoxious matters put in her way, she will be a good mother.' Judge Scott said that if Brando and Miss Kashfi, who are divorced, cannot agree on the actor's visitation days, the court would make the orders.[49]

The custody battles over Christian would not erupt again for another six years but it's clear, from Alice Marchak's account of her friendship with Brando, that it was not only Kashfi who suffered from addictive behaviour during this period. Marchak, who began working for Brando in 1958 and remained part of his life until he died, realised early on that he took amphetamines to try to control his appetite (he was also bulimic but he didn't tell her that) and 'other prescription drugs':

When I first began to work for Marlon at his house, he had a 'ready to take on the world' attitude. He whistled around the house, he sang, he played the bongos. We had funny, sometimes ridiculous conversations. He was very affable, charming, outgoing. The amphetamines and uppers and downers he told me he was taking to keep his weight in check did not seem to put him to bed in a stupor for a week at a time. The time he spent in bed was with women.[50]

Marlon Brando was from a family of addicts. His parents were both alcoholics, as was his sister Jocelyn. Brando's addictions included prescription drugs – painkillers, tranquilisers and sedatives – as well as food and sex. According to Marchak, 'Sex more than any other thing ruled his life. And ruined it.'[51] Christian Brando, in turn, would inherit his parents' compulsive behaviour. The chaotic, fractured childhood he endured produced a difficult, manipulative child who grew into a troubled, out-of-control adult who was himself addicted to drugs.

In 1972, when Christian was thirteen, perhaps the most traumatic and ruinous episode of his childhood took place. Biographer Stefan Kanfer described it as 'the squalid, the scandalous, and the odious':

> In the latter stages of filming *Last Tango*, Marlon learned that while Anna Kashfi had further descended into a haze of pills and alcohol, Christian's litany of behavioural problems ranged from substance abuse, to attacking classmates, to setting fire to a dorm at his private school in California. And now he had vanished. Anna claimed to know nothing about the youth's disappearance. In fact she knew everything. Afraid that Marlon would try and gain custody of Christian, she had arranged to have the boy spirited out of the States and into Mexico.[52]

Charles Higham, another Brando biographer, was equally appalled and referred to the episode as a 'lurid and unsavoury'.[53] There were, unsurprisingly, several sides to the story – but what appears to be indisputable is that Kashfi left her thirteen-year-old son with a group of people he had never met before across the border in Mexico and then made her way back to Los Angeles. Her reasoning was that she felt that Christian had become increasingly alienated from her following the bitter custody battles of 1965. Along with her 'deepening depression', Kashfi was distressed about his problems at school and what she perceived to be her ex-husband's negative influence and 'resolved to extricate him from that vortex'.[54] Seven years after the incident she gave her account of what happened in *Brando for Breakfast*. She had planned to take Christian for a short holiday in Mexico to cure a bout of bronchitis he had suddenly developed when she took him out of school for the weekend. He ended up travelling with friends of a friend and Kashfi arranged to meet them a few days later. When they didn't appear, she and another friend got on a bus back to Los Angeles 'Giselle and I had carried a few cans of beer on to the bus at Calexico and, drinking, we must have become a bit unruly. The driver stopped the bus and summoned police who deposited us in the nearest jail'. After Kashfi was charged with 'disturbing the peace' and being 'under the influence' she reported that her son had been kidnapped.[55] Brando flew in from France, where he was filming *Last Tango in Paris*, to oversee the search. Three days later Christian was found in a tent in the Mexican desert and reunited with his father. Kashfi, meanwhile, filed assault and battery charges against Brando and the people who worked for him after she was released from jail. Brando sued for sole custody of Christian – and won. As Kashfi later wrote: 'I was left with nothing'.[56]

For virtually the entire time that Kashfi and Brando fought over their son, they also battled their own addictions. Kashfi's were exposed repeatedly in courtrooms and newspaper reports, and later in the Brando biographies. In time they became all that she was remembered for. And what of the drugs she was prescribed throughout the decades? Barbiturates have been largely replaced by benzodiazepines, and Valium took the place of Miltown. Phenobarbital is still prescribed, although less frequently, for epilepsy and is now considered by some clinicians to be a 'dirty drug' due to the danger in some patients of adverse side effects. Alcohol, the oldest recreational medication of them all, continued to keep Kashfi company for many years.

When she published her autobiography in 1979, Kashfi stated that she had never had epilepsy and that drugs such as Librium, Tylenol and phenobarbital had been prescribed for her 'needlessly and perhaps incompetently' but nobody much cared.[57] And the newspapers who had reported every misstep along the way only wanted stories from her about Brando and his alleged sexual excesses. With little else to occupy her time, she occasionally obliged.

Notes

[1] Andrea Tone, *The Age of Anxiety: A History of America's Turbulent Affair with Tranquilizers*, (Basic Books, 2009), p. 28.

[2] *Los Angeles Herald Examiner*, 8 December 1964.

[3] Anna Kashfi & E.P. Stein, *Brando's Bride*, (Crown Publishing, 1979), p. 102.

[4] Andrea Tone, *The Age of Anxiety: A History of America's Turbulent Affair with Tranquilizers*, p. 27.

[5] Ibid.; Alice Marchak, *Me and Marlon*, (Bookmasters, 2008), p. 169.

[6] Andrea Tone, *The Age of Anxiety: A History of America's Turbulent Affair with Tranquilizers*, p. 37; Benedict Carey, 'Frank Berger, 94, Miltown Creator Dies', *New York Times*, 21 March 2008.

[7] Andrea Tone, *The Age of Anxiety: A History of America's Turbulent Affair with Tranquilizers*, p. 35.

[8] Ibid., p. 54.

[9] Andrea Tone, *The Age of Anxiety: A History of America's Turbulent Affair with Tranquilizers*, p. 55.

[10] Ibid.; Alice Marchak, *Me and Marlon*, p. 169.

[11] Andrea Tone, *The Age of Anxiety: A History of America's Turbulent Affair with Tranquilizers*, p. 56.

[12] Tessa Johnson, 'How to be a Domestic Goddess: Housewives, tranquiliser use and the nuclear family in Cold War America', 25 February 2013. https://wellcomehistory. wordpress.com/2013/02/25/how-to-be-a-domestic-goddess/

[13] Andrea Tone quoted in Benedict Carey 'Frank Berger, 94, Miltown Creator Dies', *New York Times*, 21 March 2008.

[14] Olivia Laing, *The Trip to Echo Spring*, (Cannongate Books, 2014), p. 141.

[15] Caroline Richmond, 'Frank Berger: Inventor of the first tranquilliser', *Independent*, 9 June 2008.

[16] Hadley Meares, 'The Tragic Story of Barbara La Marr, the Woman who was Too Beautiful for Hollywood', *LA Weekly*, 10 February 2017.

[17] E. J. Fleming, *The Fixers*, (McFarland & Company, 1954), p. 66.

[18] Mark Borkowski, *The Fame Formula*, (Sidgwick & Jackson, 2008), p. 140.

[19] Gerald Clarke, *Get Happy: The Life of Judy Garland*, (Sphere, 2001), p. 422.

[20] Les Iverson, *Drugs: A Very Short Introduction*, (Oxford University Press, 2016), p. 90; Leslie Iverson, *Speed, Ecstasy, Ritalin: The Science of Amphetamines*, (Oxford University Press, 2006), p. 102.

[21] Alan Jacobs, 'The Lost World of Benzedrine', *The Atlantic*, 15 April 2012.

[22] Leslie Iverson, *Speed, Ecstasy, Ritalin: The Science of Amphetamines*, p. 103.

[23] Anna Kashfi, *Brando for Breakfast*, p. 126.

[24] Cari Beauchamp and Judy Balaban, 'Cary in the Sky with Diamonds', *Vanity Fair*, August 2010.

[25] *Daily Mirror*, 23 April 1959.

[26] *Daily Mirror*, 15 December 1959.

[27] *Daily Express,* 10 December 1959.

[28] Ibid.

[29] *Empire News*, 13 December 1959.

[30] *Winnipeg Free Press*, 16 December 1959.

[31] *Daily Mirror*, 22 December 1959.

[32] Anna Kashfi, *Brando for Breakfast*, p. 153.

[33] Charles Higham, *Brando: The Unauthorized Biography*, (New American Library, 1987), p. 207.

[34] Anna Kashfi, *Brando for Breakfast*, p. 154.

[35] Beverley Linet, *Star Crossed: The Story of Robert Walker and Jennifer Jones*, (G. P. Putnam's Sons, 1985), pp. 268-271.

[36] Anna Kashfi, *Brando for Breakfast*, p. 193.

[37] *Los Angeles Herald Examiner*, 8 December 1964.

[38] Anna Kashfi, *Brando for Breakfast*, p. 194.

[39] *Los Angeles Herald Examiner*, 8 December 1964.

[40] Ibid.

[41] Anna Kashfi, *Brando for Breakfast*, p. 194.

[42] Charles Higham, *Brando: The Unauthorized Biography*, p. 240.

[43] *Long Beach Press*, 5 January 1965.

[44] Anna Kashfi, *Brando for Breakfast*, p. 195.

[45] Ibid., p. 196.

[46] Ibid.

[47] Ibid., p. 198.

[48] Ibid., p. 199.

[49] *The Albuquerque Tribune*, 2 October 1965.

[50] Alice Marchak, *Me and Marlon*, p. 169, p. 173.

[51] Ibid., p. 5.

[52] Stefan Kanfer, *Somebody: The Reckless Life and Remarkable Career of Marlon Brando*, (Faber and Faber, 2008), p. 256.

[53] Charles Higham, *Brando: The Unauthorized Biography*, (New American Library, 1987), p. 279.

[54] Anna Kashfi, *Brando for Breakfast*, pp. 241-242.

[55] Ibid., p. 245.

[56] Ibid., p. 246.

[57] Ibid., p. 272.

12

Spider Bites Actress

Miss Anna Kashfi, the actress and former wife of Marlon Brando, is recovering from the bite of a deadly brown recluse spider. Miss Kashfi, who is 38, has undergone skin grafts on her right ankle.

The Times, December 8 1972

Anna, the girl who lied for love, pops up again

Daily Express, August 16 1978

In 1972, when Kashfi lost custody of her son for the last time, she entered her wilderness years. For the next four and a half decades she would exist, in public, largely as a footnote in Marlon Brando's life story. Privately she rattled around California acquiring another husband, a ghost-written autobiography and a job as a care-worker in an old people's home. There was also a painful role as an absent spectator during her son's murder trial in the 1990s. Perhaps she was lucky? After all neither Belinda Lee, Pier Angeli nor Gia Scala were afforded much of an afterlife – a life *after* the journalists stopped calling, the career was exorcised and the face no longer resembled that of a twenty-year-old. Their misfortunes were done and dusted in ten or so years, at most. Kashfi's went on and on – and on.

On January 1974, sixteen years after leaving Brando, she married again. For the ceremony Kashfi headed to Las Vegas and a place known as 'The Miracle in the Desert'.[1] Built in 1955, the iconic Dunes was the tenth hotel to open in what was then a dusty town in Nevada but would soon become the entertainment capital of the world. In its heyday the Dunes hosted performers like Sinatra, Judy Garland and Dean Martin. It was the first hotel to put on a topless revue and it also boasted the largest swimming pool in America – and yet still struggled to be profitable. By the time Kashfi arrived there in the early 1970s the Dunes was way past its best. Still, somehow, the hotel staggered on for another twenty years until finally it was blown up, Las Vegas-style, with a million dollars-worth of fireworks. It was a blowsy, big-hearted adieu – kicking off the 'implosion craze' – a very Vegas way of disposing of a financial liability.[2]

It wasn't only the location and the husband that were different second time around. There is a photograph of the newlyweds cutting the cake and, unlike the funereal expressions in the Brandos marriage portrait, both the bride and groom are laughing. In fact, Kashfi is scarcely recognisable as the moody-looking beauty of the 1950s – and not just because she is approaching her fortieth birthday. There was, back then, a wistfulness about her (which her son inherited in his teenage years), and it is that which has disappeared. The second husband was also an older man, rumoured to be between six and fifteen years her senior. James (Jim) Hannaford has been variously described as a Los Angeles businessman, vice president of an electronics firm and a piped-music salesman – all, perhaps, different ways of describing the same job. Kashfi was still called an actress – despite the fact that she had not acted for at least a decade.

At the time of her first wedding Kashfi was pregnant with Christian. In Las Vegas the by now fifteen-year-old boy was there again. This time acting as a surrogate father and giving his mother away. Or so Manso claimed in his biography of Brando.[3] Strangely, Kashfi makes no mention of this symbolic act, which surely suggested a reconciliation of sorts with her child, in her autobiography – but she did say this:

> Marlon telephoned on wedding's eve to extend his congratulations to us both. The following day he told a friend, 'Damn! Now I'll never get her committed.'[4]

She also failed to reveal that Brando had had her prospective husband followed for several weeks prior to the wedding by his private detective, Jay Armes.

Hannaford had two sons, Kyle and Cary, either side of Christian in age, who were also at the wedding. Kashfi, no longer allowed to bring up her own child, had acquired someone else's. Yet, despite this new-found domestic stability, a month after the wedding she again attempted suicide – laying the blame for the moment 'when I nearly died' firmly at Brando's door.[5] She related a conversation that she said took place:

> It was Valentine's Day. Marlon had telephoned: 'Now I've got you down where you deserve to be. All I have to do is kick dirt into your grave.' I had sworn at him in return, but the exchange still rankled.[6]

And so she 'took a few pills, neither more nor less than on other occasions when pressures from Marlon became overwhelming'.[7]

It's an odd and possibly suspect account, given Brando's preoccupations at this time. While Kashfi spent the beginning of 1974 getting married and being hospitalised for an overdose, Brando was mostly out of town, in St Paul, Minnesota. He was attending the trials of Dennis Banks and Russell Means – American Indian activists who had played a prominent role in the seventy-one day standoff between the American Indian Movement (AIM) and the Federal authorities in the town of Wounded Knee the previous year.[8] Throughout the 1960s, Brando had pledged his allegiance to various causes, predominantly the Civil Rights Movement of which he was a long-time supporter. Harry Belafonte, a close friend of Martin Luther King Jr., recruited a number of Hollywood stars alongside Brando including Paul Newman, Charlton Heston and Burt Lancaster. Brando was keen on using direct action to further the cause and suggested a group of actors chain themselves to the Jefferson Memorial and lie down in front of the White House. Heston refused and demanded that they all obey the law.[9] Thwarted in that attempt, it was left to the Oscars to provide Brando's most controversial political moment. Following his nomination for Best Actor for his role in *The Godfather* in March 1973 he sent the Native American activist, Sacheen Littlefeather, to the Dorothy Chandler Pavilion to represent him.[10] Meanwhile, he watched the ceremony on television at home in Mulholland Drive with Christian and another son, Miko, At that time the blockade at Wounded Knee, a tiny village within the desolate Pine Ridge Native Indian reservation in South Dakota, was nearly halfway through the seventy-one day dispute which would make it the longest lasting act of civil disobedience in American history. Between February and May 1973 more than two hundred Native American Indians and some followers seized and then occupied the town of Wounded Knee. The protest ended after two deaths, numerous injuries, countless meetings and a last minute gunfight when a hundred members of the American Indian Movement surrendered and left the town.[11] When Brando's name was announced as the winner by Liv Ullman and Roger Moore, Sacheen Littlefeather walked onto the stage to wave away the Oscar.

Brando's contentious rejection of the statuette, on the grounds that the film and television industries' portrayal of Native American Indians was offensive, was in marked contrast to his apparent delight at winning his first Oscar for *On the Waterfront*. On that occasion, a youthful-looking Brando had skipped smartly up onto the stage to accept the award from Hollywood grande-dame Bette Davis, who was resplendent in a bejewelled pixie hat. After Miss Davis had shaken him firmly by the hand and told him he was 'just *great*', Brando addressed the audience.[12] His manner was reminiscent of how George Englund described him speaking to Kashfi the first time they met in the Paramount commissary, 'a little urbanity, a little shy guy, a touch of European inflection, a soupçon of British good manners, no vulgarity, no Wild One'[13]:

[Feeling the weight of the Oscar] It's much heavier than I imagined... Gosh, I had something to say and I can't remember what I was going to say for the life of me.... I don't think that ever in my life have so many people been so directly responsible for my being so very, very glad. It's a wonderful moment, and a rare one, and I'm certainly indebted. Thank-you.[14]

This courteous acknowledgement belied the fact that Brando, according to Budd Schulberg, screenwriter of *On the Waterfront*, thought awards were just 'self-congratulary nonsense' and it was Schulberg and the boxer Roger Donoghue, who trained Brando for Terry Malloy's fight scenes, who had persuaded him to attend:

> He accepted his best actor award with grace and a million-dollar smile. Years later he would look back on that concession as a great mistake and consequently scorn acting awards for the rest of his life.[15]

Whatever drama had gone on behind the scenes, the handover looked like a neat bridge between the old Hollywood guard and the new. In reality a regal Bette Davis and the young and handsome Brando had more in common than a first glance suggested. Both were rebels who fought the Hollywood factory system tooth and nail. Both were damaged by the fight but went on to achieve legendary status. They became icons – a position very few stars achieve. The year of Brando's first Oscar success was the same year that he met Kashfi and his 'shy-guy' acceptance speech is a rare opportunity to glimpse the charismatic, likeable man she would meet in the studio canteen some seven months later. Eighteen years after that, Brando's career was back on a high with *The Godfather* and *Last Tango in Paris* (for which he would receive another 'best actor' nomination the following year) but his concerns now lay elsewhere. It's hard to equate the thoughtful activist with someone who would behave in the way Kashfi describes.

After spending four days in a coma Kashfi survived her suicide attempt. And that is where her story ends in her autobiography, although it wouldn't be published for another five years. 'The years of turmoil have given way to a time of relative tranquillity,' she declared.[16] Not quite.

Within months of Kashfi coming out of hospital, Christian was arrested for possession of marijuana. He was sixteen years old. By now his relationship with his father, as well as his mother, was complicated and fractious; Carmine De Benedittis, a film producer who worked with Brando observed:

> When I went to meet Marlon, I noticed that when Christian is near his father, he seems to shrink, he becomes a gnat. He seems to be crushed by the force of his father's character. It's a very heavy load, to be called Christian Brando.[17]

Christian acquired habits which he would never be able to shake. He was the child of addicts with volatile temperaments and eventually it took a toll. He warned an anxious Alice Marchak early on, 'Don't waste your time on me. I'm always going to drink beer and smoke marijuana until the day I die'.[18] And so he did – at least until he moved on to the harder stuff. He was often absent from Cal Prep, the new private school Brando had enrolled him in. Cal Prep was the California Preparatory School in the Encino suburb of Los Angeles, a small, private establishment not far from Mulholland Drive. Christian left the school in 1976, the same year as his already famous classmate, Michael Jackson. Steve Hunio was a close friend of Christian's at that time. He remembered a boy who loved nature, animals and his dogs – and had an explosive temper: 'I think a lot of his anger was directed against himself. I think what was really going on was that he didn't know who he was because of his problems with his father'.[19] Other school friends remembered a horrific car accident in the canyon, when the boys must have been around sixteen or seventeen years old and Steve Hunio lost control of the car and hit the mountain. It was Christian (and another friend, Kit Braun) who got Hunio to the hospital immediately, swift action which saved his life – but neither Kashfi nor the Brando biographers mention this traumatic incident.[20]

After Christian left Cal Prep, Kashfi went back to court to file a two-million-dollar lawsuit against Brando claiming that he had kept her from seeing her son for the previous two years. She admitted that Christian was now nineteen, 'so technically, he's his own man, not controlled by anyone', but stressed she was referring to the time when he was still a minor and 'Marlon began denying me the right to see him'. She maintained she had last heard from him when he 'was on an island in the Pacific'.[21] This, presumably, was Tetiaroa, the atoll in Tahiti owned by the Tahitian royal family until they gave it to Johnson Walter Williams, the only dentist on the island. It was a descendant of Williams who sold the atoll to Brando in the 1960s when he fell in love with it while looking for locations for *Mutiny on the Bounty*. Tetiaroa was Brando's South Seas bolt-hole during the years he lived intermittently with his wife Tarita and their children, Teihotu and Cheyenne. Now and then Christian also spent time there with his half-siblings and his stepmother.

When the lawsuit came to nothing Kashfi turned to a project she had first mentioned during an interview in 1977. She revealed that she had collaborated on a book about Brando but had then withdrawn her approval after reading the manuscript and had concentrated instead on endorsing a restaurant specialising in Indian food. Two years later she changed her mind: *Brando for Breakfast*, co-authored by E.P. Stein, was published in 1979. Stein was better known as Richard A. Epstein, the author of a classic book on gambling and its mathematical analysis, *The Theory of Gambling and Statistical Logic*. Dr Epstein also worked for various American space and missile ventures for many years. Quite how he was selected to co-write Kashfi's eccentric and largely impenetrable autobiography is unclear. In the preface Kashfi herself (perhaps) tries to explain why she wrote it:

> It seemed as if I had never come to the United States, never had an acting career, never met Marlon Brando, never was pregnant, gave birth, or nurtured a child. To reassure myself of the reality of these events, I forced myself to relive them – to replay them in the mind's projection room. I have recorded that replay in the form of this book.[22]

As a memoir it is unreliable chiefly because, for reasons best known to herself, Kashfi decided that twenty years after the 'Anna: Yes, I *am* from Cardiff' headlines she would muddy the water all over again:

> An unregistered alliance between my father, Devi Kashfi, a professional architect, and my mother, Selma Ghose, brought me into the world at a time of mounting British-Indian conflict. When I was two, my mother espoused an Englishman, William Patrick O'Callaghan, thereby provoking disapproval from her family. Marriage to an Englishman was then, to many, an upward step to social prestige. To others with more nationalist fervor, it was a censurable act. Because of our familial discord and because of social unrest in the cities, both arising from the clash of two cultures, my half-brother, Bosco (two and a half years younger), and I were removed to the mountain redoubt of Darjeeling in the north of India. There I attended school at the Kurseong Roman Catholic convent.[23]

Just like the studio bios which the Paramount and MGM publicity departments had concocted on her behalf back in the 1950s, there is a grain of truth in this. Kashfi did attend the Kurseong Roman Catholic convent while Bosco went to St Joseph's College, Northpoint in Darjeeling – but he was her brother not her half-brother, her only sibling of any description in fact. She also notes, 'My mother and stepfather had taken up residence in Ogmore-by-Sea, a small resort town on the coast of Wales, close enough to afford occasional visits' but makes no mention of the family's move to Cardiff where they lived from 1949 onwards.[24] Minor details, perhaps, but they were compounded by more major fabrications: 'At eighteen I was packed off to England to the London University of Economics' which was followed by a romance with the 'irresistible, suave, charming Italian Rico Mandiaco' (but no mention of the Italian jet pilot, Franco Fatigati, who Louella Parsons named in her column in 1956). While in Paris with Rico, strolling down the Rue de la Paix, Kashfi apparently bumped into her father although they were so 'disconcerted' they didn't speak to each other. There was, however, an unfortunate consequence to this imaginary encounter which she described in a curiously Dickensian tone: 'Upon arriving back in London I found my allowance to have been precipitately severed. Thus ended my academic career.'[25]

And of course there was the strange story about the murder of Devi Kashfi (which, eerily foreshadowed the real-life murder that would blight her family thirty odd years later):

An evening later I learned that my father had died. My half-brother, Bosco, called from New Delhi to notify me. According to Bosco, he had been fatally shot; the body cremated a few hours later without an autopsy. If Bosco knew more of the mystery, he wouldn't tell me. I never learned further details of my father's death. He was forty-nine years old. We had been close in spirit although separated by distance. He had telephoned me a month previous to advise against marrying Marlon: 'He's a bum. I don't care if he is famous, he's still a bum.' I had slammed the phone down on him for his impertinence.

Now I couldn't reason with him. He was beyond regrets.
I felt giddy, with a sensation of falling in space.[26]

Was Kashfi's revisiting of her fake Hollywood biography
a deliberate decision to reclaim the persona she had constructed during her happiest times with Brando? Or had
she simply travelled so far from Joan O'Callaghan over
the past quarter of a century that she couldn't find a way
back to her? Whatever her reasons, the book is an un-
comfortable brew: a bizarre analysis of Brando's film roles
intercut with salacious details about his sex life. American
gossip columnist, Rona Barratt, (a successor of Hopper
and Parsons) reviewed the book and pronounced it a 'ven-
omous exposé' and that she 'loved it' – a quote the
publishers were happy to use on the cover of the paper-
back edition.[27]

With her ex-husband still her most lucrative asset and
the stern-faced, but still-handsome, Brando adorning her
book jacket Kashfi gamely embarked upon a promotional
tour. 'Branded Brando' reported the *Daily Express*: 'He
made our home a love-nest – but not for me, says his ex-
wife Anna'.[28] In one interview, with the Hollywood
Drama-Logue in October 1979, the journalist David
Galligan refers to her 'great moon eyes' and sad smile
when, as he puts it, 'we get to the Brando questions'.[29]

There is no record of what William O'Callaghan, still
living in the Newfoundland Road house in Cardiff, thought
of the book. He died two years later at the age of eighty-
two in the city he had made his home during what must
have been the unhappiest decades of his life. Phoebe
O'Callaghan, who was entirely eradicated from Kashfi's

autobiography, just as she was in 1957, had been dead for fifteen years at the time of publication.

In May 1990, six days after his thirty-second birthday, Christian Brando shot Dag Drollet in the face at close range while the latter watched television in Marlon Brando's Mullholland Drive home. Dag Drollet, the son of a Tahiti Government official, was Cheyenne Brando's boyfriend and the father of her unborn child. Brando had invited Cheyenne and Dag to stay with him while the heavily-pregnant Cheyenne received psychiatric help in Los Angeles following a bad car crash. She was twenty, a sometime model and full-time drug-user. Her relationship with Dag was complicated. He was apparently trying to extricate himself from the Brando clan and there was another young woman in Tahiti who was also pregnant with his child. Dag's father, Jacques Drollet, told the Los Angeles Times two months after the killing that he had tried to warn his son about Cheyenne:

> I said you're going to meet a tragedy with that girl, your life together smells of tragedy, it smells of death.[30]

The story of that evening which came to be told was that Christian and Cheyenne had gone out for dinner at the Musso and Frank Grill on Hollywood Boulevard, a restaurant famous for its association with literary figures including Scott Fitzgerald, Dorothy Parker, John Steinbeck, Aldous Huxley and Raymond Chandler. Allegedly, during the meal, Cheyenne told Christian that Dag sometimes hit her.[31] On the way back to Mullholland Drive, Christian stopped off at his girlfriend Laurene Langdon's house to pick up some beers, a knife and a handgun. He showed the weapon to Cheyenne. 'It was so light I thought it was a toy,' she would later recall.[32] When he arrived at his father's home, Christian and Dag began to argue. One shot was heard. Brando ran in from another part of the house and found his son with the gun in his hand and Dag sprawled on the white sofa – cigarette papers and a lighter in one hand, the TV remote control in the other. There was a gunshot wound the size of a ten pence coin in his cheek. After attempting, unsuccessfully, to revive Dag, Brando called the police. They arrived to find Christian sitting on a bedroom floor with his arm around Cheyenne, crying. 'Man, I didn't mean to shoot him,' he told the police. 'He fought for the gun; we were rolling around on the couch. I told him to let go. He had my hands, then boom'.[33]

Two days later, Christian was charged with first-degree murder. Six days after Dag's death, on 22nd May, Brando attended the first bail hearing with three of his children (he had nine by this time) and Cheyenne's mother, Tarita. After failing to secure his son's release Brando put his house up as security and, three months later, a $2 million-dollar bail was agreed. When Christian strolled out of the Men's Central Jail in Los Angeles, hands in his pockets, his sixty-six-year-old father was by his side – and the press were waiting:

Brando Is Released From Jail: Murder case: Actor's son is met by a crowd of photographers and reporters. The slaying suspect is accompanied home by family members, girlfriend and pet dog. 'I just want to go home and try to straighten this out'.[34]

210

Brando told the journalists, 'I am proud to have my son out of jail. Right now we're just going to go home and relax and do whatever Christian wants'. Christian was seen to wipe away a tear before getting in one of the two cars that were ferrying the Brando family around. En route back to the house he stopped for two hamburgers and a root beer.[35]

There was no sign of Kashfi. Instead, she issued a statement in which she laid the blame for the tragedy firmly at the door of her ex-husband. 'The person who should be in jail, the man who should be in the dock with his hands cuffed is Marlon Brando not my son.'[36]

Brando hired a lawyer named Robert (Bob) Shapiro to defend his son. Still four years away from the central role he would play in the so-called Dream Team which defended O.J. Simpson, it was Shapiro's successful plea-bargaining in the Christian Brando case which was to make him famous. The sharp-suited Shapiro had a reputation for getting celebrities out of trouble. His line of defence for Christian was that he was trying to protect his sister from an abusive boyfriend. In order to challenge that, the prosecution needed Cheyenne to give evidence against her half-brother. She had already provided an alternative version of what happened on the night that Dag died, describing a short argument and then a gunshot, which tallied with the evidence at the crime scene – thus contradicting Christian's account of a lengthier struggle for control of the gun. But, three days after her police interview, Cheyenne went home to Tahiti with her mother and refused all requests to return and testify. Her son, Tuki, was born prematurely on 26th June, six weeks after

Dag's death. Shapiro, meanwhile, continued to draw attention to Cheyenne's mental instability: 'This is a seriously disturbed young woman. She has changed her story five times.'[37] This was backed up by Brando who agreed that she was in no condition to appear in court. When Cheyenne attempted suicide three months later, in October 1990, Shapiro negotiated a deal in which Christian was allowed to plead guilty to the lesser charge of manslaughter. For Cheyenne, life only got worse. She lost custody of her son, Tuki, and, in April 1995, hanged herself at her mother's house at the age of twenty-five. Brando would not forgive her and when he died, nine years after his daughter, he specifically excluded Tuki from his will.[38]

When Christian's sentencing hearing finally came up in February 1991, Brando pleaded for leniency for his son in front of the eighty people in the courtroom in a lengthy speech which was reported around the world. He spoke for over an hour, sometimes sobbing, sometimes raging ('the plain man's Lear' as one newspaper called him), admitting that Christian was 'a basket case of emotional disorders' by the time he was thirteen.[39] He said that he had only married Kashfi because she was pregnant and because he didn't want the child to grow up 'an internationally-famous illegitimate son'. He also said this about the woman he lived with briefly – and fought at length:

> While Shapiro led him through the peaks and valleys of Brando's marriage to Christian's mother, Anna Kashfi, who was not in the courtroom, Marlon mentioned her temper, instability and attractiveness. 'She was probably

the most beautiful woman I've ever known, but she came close to being as negative a person as I have met in my life.' Still, he shouldered much of the blame: 'I led a wasted life. I chased a lot of women. Perhaps I failed as a father. The tendency is always to blame the other person. There were things I could have done differently'.

And, finally he cried:

'I did the best I could'.[40]

The performance, however genuine, did not save his son. Christian was sentenced to ten years in the California Men's Colony – a state prison in San Luis Obispo midway between Los Angeles and San Francisco. Just before he was led away to begin his sentence, the man who had met their son no more than a handful of times before he killed him, turned and addressed the Drollet family, 'It is not my family's fault, it is mine. If I could trade places with Dag I would'.[41]

Christian died four years after his father at the age of forty-nine. The obituaries said that Kashfi, who was at his bedside in the Hollywood Presbyterian Medical Centre as he lay in a coma for fifteen days, had not seen him for twenty years. It's hard to know if this is true or not – but it's safe to speculate that, at best, they were estranged. After he left jail, having served less than half of his decade-long sentence, Christian had thirteen years of his life left to live. Several of them were spent in Kalama, a small town in Washington State around a thousand miles from Los Angeles. Trying to make a living as a welder but traumatised by the shooting, the trial and his time in prison, Christian became seriously addicted to 'crystal meth' (methamphetamine).[42] After Brando's death in 2004, he moved back to Los Angeles. No longer able to live at his father's Mulholland Drive house after it was sold to next door neighbour Jack Nicholson, the son who had tried to make a life for himself both in and out of his father's shadow was now catastrophically adrift. In January 2008, by now a destitute addict, Christian was admitted to hospital with pneumonia. When he died, the newspaper in the city Kashfi hadn't lived in since she was seventeen had a new headline: 'Brando's Cardiff Wife Loses Her Troubled Son' in the 'latest tragic episode for actor's forgotten ex'.[43]

James Hannaford died in 1986. In 1979, while promoting *Brando for Breakfast*, Kashfi told David Galligan that when she had met Hannaford she was a 'total wreck' and that 'through Jim I've pulled everything together'. By 1992, six years after Hannaford's death,

Kashfi appeared to have fallen on hard times. No longer living in Los Angeles, a journalist tracked her down to a small town called Alpine, thirty miles from San Diego, where, according to the South Wales Echo, she was now 'living in a dingy caravan':

> Once she was married to Brando and enjoyed the life of a princess in Hollywood. Now, she's living on £30 a week. Ex-South Wales schoolgirl Anna Kashfi who once lived the life of luxury as the wife of a Hollywood superstar is today alone and penniless...[44]

The article is accompanied by a photograph of Kashfi staring balefully at the camera. She is unlike the previous Kashfis we have seen over the years. 'I've come down a lot and learned to live on nothing,' she said. The article went on to reveal that 'When asked about her Welsh background, she denied ever having been to Wales, or to have gone to St Joseph's Convent School in North Road, Cardiff. Her parents, who were heartbroken that their daughter could deny their existence, are now both dead.' Despite Kashfi's 'world record settlement' from Brando, she was now 'scrubbing and cleaning in an old folks home for a little extra money'. Kashfi is the fallen princess – indeed according to the newspaper she had 'claimed to have been a princess born in Calcutta'. Now, like Cinderella in reverse, she has gone from riches to rags.

When the death of Marlon Brando was announced, in July 2004, Kashfi was once again in demand. How strange it must have been to hear that he was gone. Jocelyn, ('Tiddy'), the surviving sister who had been friendly with Kashfi all those years before, was with him in the UCLA Medical Centre ; 'he just took off... He's off on his trip, whatever that is...'. she said.[45] George W. Bush's White House issued a rare statement:

> America has lost a great actor of the stage and screen. His award-winning performances in films such as On the Waterfront and The Godfather demonstrated his outstanding talent and entertained millions across the country. Marlon Brando was one of the 20th century's finest actors and will be missed by his many fans and admirers.[46]

Sixty-nine-year-old Kashfi was neither a fan nor an admirer – a point she made abundantly clear when she told a newspaper that she wished that she had never met him: 'The world may be mourning the loss of a brilliant actor but personally he was a monster'.[47] For Kashfi it was like turning back the clock forty years; once again she could be the angry ex-wife – and naturally she delivered. It was what they paid her to do. In return Budd Schulberg called her a 'violent, vindictive drunk'.[48] Kashfi now seemed convinced that, with Brando out of the way, her relationship with her child would finally be restored: 'the only good thing that has come out of his passing is that Christian and I can now meet again openly as mother and son and I can give him some of the love that has been missing all these years'.[49] It looked like a forlorn hope – both mother and child had had years to create whatever relationship they wanted to have. It was a sad irony that, just as Kashfi had no connection with her parents as an adult, neither did her son with her.

On the 30th June 2005, on the eve of the first anniversary of Brando's death, the New York branch of Christies Auction House held a sale of his possessions. *The Personal Property of Marlon Brando* contained three hundred and twenty-eight lots – everything from furniture to books, scripts and letters, watches and wind chimes. It was, in fact, virtually the entire contents of his Mulholland Drive home – the house he had lived in for forty-five years. Lot 150 was the one that enabled Kashfi once again to hit the headlines. The listing in the catalogue describes an item with a reserve price of between $800-1,200:

A14k gold St. Christopher circular medallion on a chain, the obverse decorated with an image of St. Christopher and inscription Saint Christopher, Protect Us, the reverse engraved DEVI BRANDO[50]

It was DEVI which marked it as a gift from mother to son. Brando had always called him Christian or Chris (Christian, in turn, called his father Bunky or Pop). To most people he was known as Chris but Kashfi had always called him Devi – the same name as her mysteriously fictitious father. 'Brando's ex-wife and son battle against New York auction of possessions,' and 'Cardiff actress demanded medallion be returned to son,' gave the impression that Christian and his mother were united in their fight against Brando's estate for an item of sentimental value.[51] Not so. Christian opposed the sale (two of Brando's eleven children, Miko and Rebecca, are thanked for their assistance in the catalogue) with his lawyer alleging, 'There are many things I don't think his father wanted sold. Christie's got first pick of the art and memorabilia while his children were still grieving'.[52] The auction house later confirmed that the St. Christopher had been returned – but declined to say whether they had also given Christian his father's correspondence with Martin Luther King Jr. which he was also said to be interested in. A representative of Brando's estate insisted that Christian and his siblings 'had nine months to inspect the items and retain what they wanted'.[53] It was, as far as Kashfi is concerned, a non-story – there is no quote from her beyond the comments she made at the time of Brando's death a year earlier.

When Christian died for some the most incongruous aspect was that Kashfi was now, once again, linked fiscally to her ex-husband:

> What is most curious and ironic in the aftermath of Christian's death is that whatever he may still be owed from Marlon's estate (which could be millions) will now go to Anna Kashfi, his mother, the person Brando hated most.[54]

Did Brando and Kashfi remain the bitterest of enemies until the end? Whether she benefitted once again from Brando's money is hard to assess – but what's clear is that she hoped to be reconciled with her son, even after his death. She moved to Kalama towards the end of her life only to have her final wish denied when Christian's first wife, Mary, who he divorced after six years of marriage in 1987, would not relinquish the burial plot she had purchased next to him. Even in her place of rest, there was no peace.

> Marlon Brando's first wife denied her dying wish to be buried next to their killer eldest child – by the son's first wife who had reserved the plot and refuses to give it up.[55]

Kashfi, still labelled by her disputed heritage ('born to a British father'), was instead buried in the plot above Christian – meaning that – 'they are head to head'.[56]

Notes

[1] Rob Ponte and Michael Lyle, *Las Vegas Sun* website, https://lasvegassun.com/history/implosions/

[2] Ibid.

[3] Peter Manso, *Brando*, (Weidenfeld & Nicolson, 1994), p. 782.

[4] Anna Kashfi & E.P. Stein, *Brando for Breakfast*, (Crown Publishers, 1979), p. 270.

[5] Ibid.

[6] Ibid.

[7] Ibid.

[8] Peter Manso, *Brando*, p. 784.

[9] Steven J. Ross, *Hollywood Left and Right*, (Oxford University Press, 2011), p. 284.

[10] Peter Manso, *Brando*, p. 774.

[11] Emily Chertoff, 'Occupy Wounded Knee: A 71-Day Siege and a Forgotten Civil Rights Movement', *The Atlantic*, 23 October 2012.

[12] 'Marlon Brando Wins Best Actor: 1955 Oscars'. https://www.youtube.com/watch?v=I_VJtDZBttY

[13] George Englund, *The Naked Brando*, (Gibson Square, 2010), p. 43.

[14] Marlon Brando Wins Best Actor: 1955 Oscars'. https://www.youtube.com/watch?v=I_VJtDZBttY

[15] Budd Schulberg, 'The King Who Would Be Man', *Vanity Fair*, 22 January 2007.

[16] Anna Kashfi, *Brando for Breakfast*, p. 272.

[17] Christopher Goodwin, 'The Boy Brando Lost', *The Observer Magazine*, 24 February 2008.

[18] Alice Marchak, *Me and Marlon*, (BookMasters, 2008), p. 315.

[19] Peter Manso, *Brando*, p. 793.

[20] Cal Prep Alumni http://www.calprepschool.com/class_ profile.cfm?member_id=3729807

[21] *Oakland Tribune*, 14 July 1977.

[22] Anna Kashfi, *Brando for Breakfast*, p. viii.

[23] Ibid., pp. 15-16.

[24] Ibid., p.17.

[25] Ibid., p.18.

[26] Ibid., p. 102.

[27] Ibid., jacket cover.

[28] *Daily Express*, 9 January 1979.

[29] *Hollywood Drama-Logue*, October 1979.

[30] *Los Angeles Times*, 28 July 1990.

[31] David Jessel, *Murder Casebook*, (Marshall Cavendish, 1994), p. 3444.

[32] Ibid., p. 3445.

[33] Ibid.

[34] *Los Angeles Times*, 16 August 1990.

[35] Ibid.

[36] David Jessel, *Murder Casebook*, p. 3453.

[37] Ibid., p. 3451.

[38] Matthew Heller, 'Brando Will Left Zilch For 2 Kids', *New York Daily News*, 10 July 2004.

[39] *The Independent*, 21 August 1990.

[40] Stefan Kanfer, *Somebody: The Reckless Life and Remarkable Career of Marlon Brando*, (Faber and Faber, 2008), p. 289.

[41] David Jessel, *Murder Casebook*, p. 3455.

[42] Christopher Goodwin, 'The Boy Brando Lost', *The Observer Magazine*, 24 February 2008.

[43] *Western Mail*, 30 January 2008.

[44] *South Wales Echo*, 28 September 1992.

[45] *The Telegraph*, 7 July 2004.

[46] Stefan Kanfer, *Somebody: The Reckless Life and Remarkable Career of Marlon Brando*, p. 308.

[47] *Western Mail*, 28 June 2005.

[48] Budd Schulberg, 'The King Who Would Be Man', *Vanity Fair*, 22 January 2007.

[49] *Western Mail*, 28 June 2005.

[50] Christie's, *The Personal Property of Marlon Brando: Thursday 30th June 2005*, (Christie's, 2005), p. 66.

[51] *Western Mail*, 28 June 2005.

[52] Ibid.

[53] Ibid.

[54] Christopher Goodwin, 'The Boy Brando Lost', *The Observer Magazine*, 24 February 2008.

[55] *Daily Mail*, 31 August 2015.

[56] Ibid.

13

'Ethnically Ambiguous' Actress Dies

Anna Kashfi, an alluring and ethnically ambiguous actress who was the first wife of Marlon Brando has died. She was 80.
Hollywood Reporter, August 25th 2015

'Sometimes I think – what happened?'
Anna Kashfi

In the spring of 2009 I visited Anna Kashfi at her home in Alpine, near San Diego, and interviewed her over several days. There is a short exchange towards the end of our final conversation which goes like this: I had asked whether she kept in touch with her agents in London, Eric and Blanche Glass, and she replied, 'Well, they're my agents. I haven't kept in touch with Glynn'. Glynn was Glynn Mortimer, the woman who in a 1959 interview with *Parade*, the weekly American magazine, claimed to have suggested her friend Joan O'Callaghan change her name to the more exotic-sounding Anna Kashfi. The interview took place more than fifty years after Kashfi had last seen Glynn and this was what she said:

As a matter of fact it was Glynn who I shared an apartment with and it was Glynn who worked for them

[Eric and Blanche Glass]. And she came home one day and said 'Hey, they need an Indian girl for a Spencer Tracy...' And I said, 'I don't know, I've never acted'. She said 'Yes, you're going to act'. Can you believe that? A little girl from Wales, originally in London and also from India. And you know all the shit that they came out with, the O'Callaghans, Marlon believed everything – he didn't believe me, he believed them and that's what hurt. And then you know, when you think about it, he and his family were from Omaha, Nebraska, what the hell did they know about it? They were farm people, they don't know anything...

Sometimes I think – what happened?[1]

In this book I have pieced together the story of the life that Anna Kashfi led in order to try and redress the casual and erroneous disregard in which she is held. Much is missing, of course, all of our lives are jigsaw puzzles with lost pieces that we work around, but in this instance I had enough information to give the shape of her life – some of *what* happened, but, so far, not *why* it happened. The leading players are Anna Kashfi (AKA Joan O'Callaghan), Marlon Brando, and the parents-in-law he never met, William and Phoebe O'Callaghan. Other significant factors include the racially-charged climate of post-war Britain, a system of colonial administration and, on a different continent again, an industry which was built upon fairy tales. What is undeniable is that the principal characters fiddled around with the truth *because* of what lay behind it. When Kashfi referred to 'all the shit that the O'Callaghans came

224

out with' she was indiscriminately, and almost certainly unknowingly, alluding to a political act created by a giant corporation (the East India Company who originally encouraged relationships between English men and Indian women) and compounded by a democratically elected ruling body (the British Government who relied upon the Anglo-Indians to oil the machinery of their rule).

It's hard not to feel some sympathy for Kashfi's parents despite the corrosive consequences of their actions. There is no evidence that they intended malice or wanted to hurt Kashfi, as she appeared to believe. They, like their daughter, had constructed a story: a hazy thumbnail sketch of how life was before they arrived in Cardiff. The problem arose only when the two stories diverged; when Kashfi concocted a different version – one that involved identifying her parents as people with Indian rather than Irish-sounding names. The story was scrutinised because Kashfi, to paraphrase the *Chicago Daily Tribune*, 'hit lightning' – and what on earth were the odds of that happening?[2] If she had not married the most famous film star in the world, the elusive, inaccessible and unattainable Marlon Brando, chances are that no reporter would ever have bothered to track down a factory worker living in Wales, to knock on his front door and to snoop and pry into his family's background. And they did pry. Three days after Kashfi married Brando, The *Los Angeles Times* reported, slyly:

> The mother, dark complexioned, became testy when asked if her daughter got her Indian blood from her, 'I'm English. I was born in London'.[3]

Just as Kashfi had backed herself into a corner, so too had her parents. Faced with a choice between their own façade crumbling, or embarrassing their daughter, they chose the latter. They could not possibly have known the long-term ramifications of that decision. They chose to insist on what they knew to be fiction; 'I'm *English*. I was born in *London*.' (Emphasis mine). Why did Mr and Mrs O'Callaghan create the equivalent of a studio-bio for their family when they were not in the movie business? I believe that the answers lie between the journey on the SS Ranchi and their life in Newfoundland Road. The O'Callaghans' arrival in Britain fell between the Royal Assent of the British Nationality Act of 1948 in July of that year and its enactment the following January. By the time William and Phoebe's daughter married Marlon Brando, in October 1957, nearly ten years had passed since the *Evening Standard* newspaper headline announced that it had chartered an aeroplane to hail the Empire Windrush with the headline 'Welcome Home! Evening Standard plane greets the 400 sons of Empire' and the warmth of that welcome had cooled somewhat.[4]

In order to understand some of what came next, it's important to recognise what came before. Little has been written about the experiences of the Anglo-Indians who lived in India as the British prepared to leave in 1947. Following years of preferential treatment under the British Raj their lives were thrown into chaos, their economic circumstances altered dramatically and some bore traumatic witness to the carnage which resulted from the severing of the continent. The personal experiences of the

O'Callaghan and Shrieves families during this time have not been recorded but, by their actions, it's clear that they followed the pattern of other Anglo-Indian families who found themselves in similar circumstances. Cliff Richard (Harry Webb) remembered it like this:

> We came to England in 1948 when the British all flooded back home after India won its independence. My parents were British, but both of them had been born abroad and neither of them had ever been to England, so they had no 'home' to come to.[5]

In fact, as Dorothy McMenamin, an Anglo-Indian born in Rawalpindi in the newly created state of Pakistan, points out in her study of the impact of Partition on the Anglo-Indians:

> It was the removal of employment privileges which had existed under the British that forced them to examine their own ambivalent position and raised concern for their future prospects. The spectre of communal rivalry between Muslims and Hindus made Anglo-Indians acutely aware that the interests of these two groups were likely to be promoted in Pakistan and India respectively after Partition. It is for these reasons that those who had the option chose to emigrate.[6]

McMenamin believes that it was because the Anglo-Indians posed no physical or economic threat to Hindus, Muslims or Sikhs 'being neither money-lenders nor wealthy landlords' that they were not the targets of violence.[7] It's clear, however, from the recollections gathered by her from people who were there at the time that, as well as observing the brutality and bloodshed in the towns, the railway workers witnessed a particular form of horror. Walter Reid describes the atmosphere in his book, *Keeping the Jewel in the Crown*:

> Between August 1947 and the spring of 1948 millions of Indians, perhaps fourteen million, perhaps sixteen million, were forced to leave their homes. No one knows the true numbers of those killed. The true figure may be around a million. But whatever the figure, the deaths alone do not speak of the horror of the times, the mutual hatred, the extravagance of the violence, rapes and mutilation. This was not the case of communities at war, Sikh, Hindu, Muslim, one seeking victory over the others. It was bloodlust, the crystallisation of hatred.[8]

Trains packed with newly displaced refugees, forced to move from one part of the country to another, would be stopped en route, usually by the placing of logs on the tracks, and the passengers taken out and slaughtered. The drivers and guards, almost always Anglo-Indian and consequently never threatened themselves, were then left to transport the train to the nearest railway station and report the massacre. Brian Birch, whose father was a train driver, said that the carnage went on for months: 'I recall my father just coming back distraught; he just didn't want to go to work. He couldn't do anything...'[9] Both William O'Callaghan and his father-in-law, Henry Shrieves, worked on the railways. William was 'Deputy Head Controller' on the Bengal Nagpur Railway and Henry was a locomotive driver; it's inconceivable that they would not have been affected in some way even if they were not on the targeted trains. Yet this was not what drove Anglo-Indians out of the only country they knew, as McMenamin reiterates:

> Despite the traumatic psychological effects of witnessing the horrendous violence, the fact that Anglo-Indians were totally excluded as targets meant the majority did not feel an immediate imperative to leave India or Pakistan because of the risk of violence. It was due to the changing climate in the employment sector after the departure of the British that they decided to emigrate.[10]

Henry Shrieves, Kashfi's grandfather, was the first in the family to take the plunge. He left India in February 1948 with his wife and four of their children six months after the British departed and just weeks after the assassination of Mahatma Gandhi in New Delhi on January 30th. The Shrieves family sailed on the Strathmore, the third of the five 'Strath Sisters'. It was the same ship which, in March 1936, had carried the new Viceroy of India, Lord Linlithgow, out to Bombay and returned with his predecessor Lord Willingdon on board. Linlithgow, known as Hopie, would spend nearly eight years in the office of Viceroy, longer than any of his post-Mutiny predecessors. Despite this it was his successor, Lord Wavell, who did what no one had expected and came up with a way out, much to the annoyance of Churchill and later Attlee (who removed Wavell from his post with the humiliatingly brief period of one month's notice). It was Wavell who had decided that India should be granted Independence within an eighteen month timeframe (believing it was either that or dig in for another thirty years) long before Mountbatten arrived.[11]

Henry Shrieves was sixty-six years old when he left his country of birth. William, the son-in-law who followed him seven months later, was twenty years younger. While the Shrieves family settled in Brighton on the south coast of England, the O'Callaghan's, William, Phoebe, Joan and Bosco, travelled cross-country into Wales at the beginning of 1949. The following April the pioneering, popular left-wing weekly magazine *Picture Post* ran the headline 'How Coloured People Live in Cardiff's Dockland' on the front cover.[12] Inside the two Berts' (Hardy and Lloyd) photographic essay, 'Down the Bay' explored the east side of Cardiff – the area known locally as the Docks or Butetown. The caption under the main photograph at the beginning of the article established the sympathetic tone:

> *Where a Housewife may Shop in Arabic with a Welsh accent: Kaid Sala's Grocery in Cardiff's Dockland.* Some 6,000 live in Bute Town, Cardiff. Most of them coloured. They live marked off from the rest of the city by social barriers, by race prejudice, and by the old Great Western Railway Bridge. They live in a community bound together by under-privilege, where the grocer's an Arab, the bootmender a Greek, where a sailor takes a drink in a Somali milk-bar or an Irish pub. It is an area with a bad name but a decent heart.[13]

In the 1950s, a researcher working in the docks recorded fifty-seven different nationalities resident in the area. Most of the immigrants were male and the women local. Tiger Bay, Butetown's nickname (apparently originating from a Portuguese sailor claiming that the waters were so dangerous to navigate that it was like sailing through a bay of tigers), became famous for both negative and positive portrayals of its multicultural residents.[14] Shirley Bassey, who worked alongside William O'Callaghan in Curran's factory, was known as 'the girl from Tiger Bay' despite the fact that she moved at an early age to the neighbouring, less glamorous sounding district of Splott.[15] No matter – her mixed-race beauty and show-stopping voice marked her out and she became the poster-girl for the Docks, the one who made it out of the grinding poverty to the very top.

But when journalists from all over the world came looking for the parents of the exotic Indian wife of Marlon Brando they didn't go 'down the bay' but instead headed four miles north of the Docks area into the (predominantly white Welsh) Gabalfa district of Cardiff. It was there that William and Phoebe struggled to maintain their version of the truth. William was, at first, in buoyant mood when discussing the mystery over his daughter giving herself an Indian name:

> If she (Anna) likes to call herself an Indian there is no reason why she should not and we are not annoyed.[16]

And then, after Kashfi's infamous honeymoon statement in which she insisted that William was her stepfather and that her mother was Indian, his tone changed. When a newspaper obtained a copy of Kashfi's baptism certificate naming both the hospital in Calcutta where she was born and both of the O'Callaghans as her parents William sounded defiant, yet wounded:

> I am glad the truth is out. Joan's mother did not want to embarrass her by proving I was her father... If she wants to forget us because we are a hindrance to her career, we will understand but I was deeply hurt when she disowned me.[17]

He may have been devastated by his daughter's insistence that he was not her biological father – but for Kashfi the exposure of her falsified parentage meant that the tentative edifice she had constructed around her new life in Los Angeles simply collapsed. Yet, if she had admitted that William's claims were true she would have revealed the artificial foundations on which the studios' stories about their stars rested. That her statement was almost certainly dictated by her employers, either Howard Strickland or Esme Chandlee in the MGM publicity department is far from coincidental.

It's hard to know what William O'Callaghan would have made of the actor Richard Burton's diary entry in November 1971 written after musing about the director John Huston's 'Eurasian' girlfriend, Zoe Sallis:

> Shades of Anna Kashfi who used to be Marlon's wife and firmly convinced him that she was Indian when it turned out – to Marlon's fury and immediate divorce – that she

was Cardiff Welsh. I knew the minute I met her just after Marlon had married her that she was Welsh and said so to her and Marlon. She affected not to know what 'Welsh' was and asked if we were like the Irish and all that kind of rubbish. Marlon wasn't interested and only became so when he found out that he'd been lied to – a heinous crime in Marlon's book. I still smile when I remember a picture of Kashfi's mother in the *Daily Express* or *Mail* with a real Celtic peasant look and wearing a 'pinny' and formidably Welsh look, sort of arms akimbo, with the caption 'Do I Look Indian?' I laughed for a week. Later I teased Marlon about it until I realized that old fatty was not inclined to regard it or her in a humorous light. I haven't tried him on that affair since. I wonder how he would take it now...[18]

Burton's casual assumption that Phoebe O'Callaghan was a 'Celtic peasant', factually incorrect of course, does raise the question of who has the right to define someone else's identity. Phoebe O'Callaghan is listed on her daughter's baptism certificate as Anglo-Indian and William O'Callaghan as Irish. Both were born in India, as were both sets of their parents. Further back, as the family tree diagram illustrates, it is more difficult to say with certainty. Was Peter O'Callaghan, William's paternal grand-father Irish by birth? Impossible to be sure, but perhaps very likely given the circumstantial evidence of the numbers of Irish men who were recruited to serve in India during that time. His mother and grandmother were both born in India – but perhaps his maternal great grand-father, Charles Boodrie, was French? Does it matter that

William and Phoebe, when asked by reporters, said that they were both born and also married in London? They knew both of those statements to be false – even if one gave them the benefit of the doubt about not knowing, or confusing the origins of their ancestors. When Mr and Mrs O'Callaghan stepped off the Ranchi at Tilbury in September 1948, they identified themselves as white British, not *Irish* and *Anglo-Indian* as they had been fourteen years earlier.

In the decade between the welcome afforded to the '400 sons of Empire' aboard the Empire Windrush in the summer of 1948 and the notorious Notting Hill riots across the August bank holiday weekend of 1958 – the extent of the unease felt by some about the numbers of immigrants arriving in Britain was laid bare. Notwithstanding the ugly language and thuggish outbursts, what is striking is the kind of behaviour that was considered an acceptable part of everyday life. In 1963 it took a boycott organised by Paul Stephenson, a youth-worker in the city, to overturn the colour bar operated by the Bristol Omnibus Company. After four months the company backed down and agreed to employ black and Asian bus crews. This case was considered influential in the passing of the Race Relations Act in 1965 which made racial discrimination unlawful in public places. Back in Cardiff, now home to the O'Callaghan family, the 'Down the Bay' article also highlighted the employment discrimination which operated freely:

Whatever their talents, precious few jobs are open to them, apart from sea-going or dock-working. For the girls, there is little chance beyond the Bute Street cafes or the rag-picking shop. Locals applying for jobs outside the dockland area are familiar with the routine treatment: the employer fears his hands will refuse to work alongside a coloured man.[19]

William O'Callaghan, a man whose job in India entitled him to a private rail carriage for the use of his family complete with his own chef, perhaps thought himself fortunate to be working as 'a checker' at Curran Steels in such a climate.[20] But, then again, as an Englishman returning from India to raise his family in the all-white district of Gabalfa he clearly identified only with the 'Anglo' part of 'Anglo-Indian'. It was his bitter misfortune that his beautiful, Indian-looking, daughter chose to identify with the other part, the Indian aspect of her heritage. Two different stories within one family.

All these instances seek to offer some understanding of the situation the O'Callaghans, like other Anglo-Indians attempting to make their homes in Britain, found themselves in. For many the concealment was absolute. In my own family, my mother only discovered that her father was Anglo-Indian nearly a quarter of a century after he had died. Yet now, as we study the photographs, we think – how could we not have known?

A curious coda to this story of lost families is the case of Rachel Dolezal; a thirty-seven-year-old black American woman who was outed as white by her parents in June 2015. *The Washington Post* ran a story comparing the Dolezal case with Kashfi's story with the headline, 'Is actress and former wife of Marlon Brando, Anna Kashfi,

Indian, British or both? No-one knows for sure'.[21] The article highlighted the apparent similarities between the two women's circumstances:

> On its face, Kashfi's story seems to parallel Dolezal's: a woman pretending to be a person of color who reached some level of prominence and was then 'outed' by her estranged parents. But while TMZ claims to have found the Spokane tanning salon responsible for Dolezal's tangerine tint, Kashfi wasn't just tan. In fact she was quite brown.[22]

Dolezal's parents were white – and so was she. The scandal was caused by the fact she had lived as a prominent black activist for a decade, her skin growing progressively darker (hence the references in the article to the tanning salon in the town she lived in) and her identification with black culture and politics complete. She put a picture of an African-American man on her Facebook page and said that he was her father. The furore that followed her parents' interview with their local newspaper in which they alleged that their daughter was Caucasian was considerable. Dolezal resigned as president of the Spokane branch of the National Association for the Advancement of Colored People, but continued to insist that she was black. The article ended with the remark, 'Kashfi's ethnicity remains a mystery and she'll probably take the truth with her to her grave'.[23]

Anna Kashfi died two months after *The Washington Post* article was published. She always knew *a* version of the truth about her origins – it's just that no one believed her. But then why else, in her words, 'would I come out like this?'[24] And what of the Brando in *Brando's Bride*? Well, in his opinion it was all, apparently, make-believe:

I made up stories about myself, including my birthplace: Calcutta, India. Later on I told Playbill I'd been born in other places – Bangkok, Thailand and Mukden, China. I have always enjoyed making up bizarre stories to see if people would believe them. Generally, they do.[25]

Notes

[1] Sarah Broughton, 'Unpublished Recorded Interviews with Anna Kashfi', April 2009.

[2] *Chicago Daily Tribune*, 19 October 1957.

[3] *Los Angeles Times*, 14 October 1957.

[4] *Evening Standard,* 22 June 1948.

[5] Cliff Richard, *My Life, My Way*, (Headline Review, 2008), p. 6.

[6] Dorothy McMenamin, 'Anglo-Indian Experiences During Partition and its Impact Upon Their Lives' *New Zealand Journal of Asian Studies* 8, 1 (June 2006), pp. 69-95.

[7] Ibid.

[8] Walter Reid, *Keeping The Jewel In The Crown*, (Birlinn, 2016), p. 1.

[9] Dorothy McMenamin, 'Anglo-Indian Experiences During Partition and its Impact Upon Their Lives' *New Zealand Journal of Asian Studies* 8, 1 (June 2006), pp. 69-95.

[10] Ibid.

[11] Walter Reid, *Keeping The Jewel in The Crown*, p. 219.

[12] A. L. Lloyd, 'Down the Bay' *Picture Post*, 22 April 1950.

[13] Ibid.

[14] Peter Hogan, *Shirley Bassey: Diamond Diva*, (Andre Deutsch, 2008), p. 15.

[15] John L. Williams, *Miss Shirley Bassey*, (Quercus, 2010), p. 34.

[16] *Mirror News*, 14 October 1957.

[17] *Chester Times*, 19 October 1957.

[18] Richard Burton, *The Richard Burton Diaries*, ed. Chris Williams, (Yale University Press, 2012), p. 530.

[19] A. L. Lloyd, 'Down the Bay', *Picture Post*, 22 April 1950.

[20] Certified Copy Of An Entry Of Death, William O'Callaghan, 25 November 1982.

[21] *The Washington Post*, 19 June 2015.

[22] Ibid.

[23] Ibid.

[24] Sarah Broughton, 'Unpublished Recorded Interviews with Anna Kashfi', April 2009.

[25] Christie's Auction Catalogue, *The Personal Property of Marlon Brando*, 30 June 2005, p. 193.

14

Finding Anna

I wanted to know how a young woman had made the journey from post-war Wales to Los Angeles to meet and marry Marlon Brando. I lived in Cardiff and frequently wandered up and down the street where Kashfi had lived as a teenager. I was absorbed in what I thought was a classic rags to riches story, but which turned out to be a complex and convoluted journey from invisibility to infamy. As I began my research I puzzled over the level of hostility she seemed to incite, particularly from the biographers of Marlon Brando. And when I set out to unravel Anna Kashfi's story I had no idea that my own grandfather was Anglo-Indian – or that Anna Kashfi's parents might have lied. These two thoughts did not even occur to me. And I had not yet met Anna Kashfi.

Meeting Anna turned out to be the travelogue part of my journey – a Californian road trip from Los Angeles to San Diego. My plan was to carry out research in the Margaret Herrick Library in Beverley Hills and roam around Kashfi's various addresses across the city. Then base myself in San Diego for a few days and commute in and out to the small town where I believed she lived. By now I had written to her twice but had received no reply. My second letter, written a couple of months after the first, explained I would be in San Diego between Saturday 4th and Wednesday 8th April and that I'd like to visit. And so I arrived on the evening of the 3rd April having travelled from Los Angeles via Cardiff-by-the-Sea, a beachside town beside the Pacific Ocean north of San Diego. The following day I would drive to Alpine, some thirty miles towards the Mexican border, and cold-call.

Around eleven o'clock in the morning I left San Diego along El Cajon Boulevard, a vast six-lane highway full of liquor stores and bathroom shops. It was sunny, hot even. Unseasonably hot for San Diego in April apparently. Beyond the city the countryside quickly became mountainous, Alpine-looking in fact. I passed Days Inns, Quality Inns and Best Westerns. Then McDonalds and WalMart and the Sycuan Resort, a Native American Reservation complete with casino. Finally I turned off for Alpine at the Tavern Road exit and immediately found myself on Alpine Boulevard. It felt like Wild West country, like something out of a movie; a settlement town. I stopped at the first place that looked inhabited – a large car park with three restaurants, a pet store and a flower shop. Every town I drove through had a pet store and, frequently, pet boutiques with clothes, accessories and grooming parlours. Alongside the pet stores there were psychics. In Los Angeles and the surrounding beach towns there were at least three psychics on every street. I bought a bunch of flowers for Anna and asked the florist where the best café was. 'Janet's is my favourite', she said. 'Or you could try The Bread Basket. They're five minutes up the road.'

I carried on along Alpine Boulevard. I knew that Anna lived at 2400 and I knew that she lived in a trailer park.

What I hadn't realised is that I didn't know which trailer. 2400 turned out to be a large piece of land with numerous mobile homes on it. She could be anywhere. Faced with the prospect of knocking on door after door, I felt momentarily defeated and went next door to 'Janet's Ranch' – a shopping area with a bunch of log cabins housing a café, a woman selling homemade bird-boxes – and a psychic. There were plenty of empty cabins with signs for antiques or no signs at all. The whole place seemed half bustling, half deserted and strangely timeless. I felt like I could have been here at any time over the past forty years and it would have looked pretty much the same. Janet's cafe looked good so I sat outside and ordered an Italian omelette and a glass of lemonade. The omelette was enormous and arrived with home fries (fried potatoes as opposed to chips) and two buttermilk scones with honey on the side. The lemonade was pink. It was another inexplicable Californian meal.

Back at 2400, I drove around until I spotted a car park with a chalet in it. It looked like an office or a centre of some sort and was deserted but, visible through one of the windows was a board with a printed list of surnames in alphabetical order on it. Next to the names were numbers. I looked for the H's and Anna was there, identifiable only by her second husband's surname. It was my first real proof that she actually existed: a strange feeling. I drove around circling large mobile homes and small mobile homes. Homes with beautiful gardens. Homes painted in pale blue and white which looked like toy homes.

Finally I found it: a brown, wooden shack with an unkempt, overgrown patch of scrubland around it. I walked up some rickety steps and onto a veranda with a door and a window with the blinds and curtains both drawn. The whole place looked closed up. Deserted. I knocked tentatively on the wooden wall and waited. Then I turned away thinking that there must be another door I can try. At the top of the steps I looked back and that's when I saw a face peering through the curtain and knew that it was Anna. I walked back and waved my flowers at her. She slid the door back a few inches with some difficulty and I explained who I was. The door opened wider and I stepped inside. I gave her the flowers and she hugged me and we stood around for a bit. We were both speechless but it felt like a happy speechless. I felt genuinely shocked that I was with the person I had dreamt of meeting for so long and she seemed faintly surprised that someone who lived in Cardiff was in her house. The room was quite chaotic and on the walls were numerous paintings, all, it turned out, painted by Anna herself. One was a view of Ogmore-by-Sea, painted from memory. She spent her first three months in Wales in Ogmore in the autumn of 1948 – a long time ago now. On the coffee table, amongst the debris, were the two envelopes with my writing on it. She offered me a glass of wine and cleared a space for me on the settee and then we sat and talked. The first thing she told me was that she was being sued by her son's ex-girlfriend and that she had a rat eating its way around her kitchen which would cost her $200 to get rid of. 'Do you hear the mouse?' she kept saying.

I had intended only to ask her for a convenient time to return and do an interview but we ended up talking for a couple of hours, maybe more. She told me she had lived in Alpine for fifteen years and that she moved here with Jim Hannaford, the second husband. She interrupted herself frequently with the same refrain 'How did a little girl from India end up in Hollywood?' She smiled as she said it. She was vague, charming, repetitive and easily distracted. I came to realise, over the three occasions that I spent time with her, that she had two fundamental pre-occupations that she repeatedly returned to: her parents' (whom she referred to as 'The O'Callaghan's') *betrayal* of her – her words. And, of course, Brando. She blamed her parents, William and Phoebe (no mention was ever made of Devi Kashfi and Selma Ghose – as if they really were entirely fictitious characters), for her marriage being destroyed because Brando believed their version of the family's history not hers which, in her view, led to her son being taken away from her and the loss of her career. She never saw her parents after she left for America in 1955. And she never forgave them.

On the Monday we went out for lunch. Anna ordered a shrimp salad and ate only the shrimps and then we returned to the house to record the interview. We did the same thing on Wednesday. Lunch in a different restaurant, same food. This time I recorded the interview in the restaurant as she was talking well, telling great stories (about her uncle Valentine dating Merle Oberon in Calcutta, about Frank Sinatra singing for two hours at an MGM party in Chasen's and Kirk Douglas having one arm shorter than the other) and I worried that if we interrupted ourselves and drove back to the house we wouldn't be able to pick up in the same way. In the end, we went shopping in a local supermarket on the way back. Anna bought carafes of wine, twenty-four cans of Coke, kitchen rolls and two tins of Shake n'Bake. When we got back to the trailer park I realised she already had twenty-four cans of Pepsi sitting on the kitchen floor – one pack of twelve kept a drawer in place while the other pack of twelve trapped the rat in a cupboard. Unfortunately the cupboard was full of food so it was probably quite happy.

Over the days I saw Anna and the nights I spoke with her on the phone I came to believe her story. Too much of it slotted into place and made sense for it not to be true and too much of it tied in with my research findings. For instance, if William O'Callaghan was born in London, as he said, why doesn't he (or his father Henry O'Callaghan) appear in either the 1901 or the 1911 census? Anna maintained her father's grandparents were born in Ireland and then travelled to India. She also said that her mother's family had been born in India, but that originally they were English which again tied in with research revealing that Phoebe was descended from John Shrieves. I had never been able to work out why they ended up in Wales when they apparently had no family connections there; William had been Head Train Controller in Adra, India before working in a factory in Cardiff so it can't have been for the job. Anna's explanation was that her mother ran a café for British servicemen in India during World War Two and that the family became very friendly with someone who came from Ogmore-by-Sea and for that reason they went there, and from there to Cardiff where William found work.

One of the most fascinating and informative parts of my conversations with Anna was about the attitudes of

Anglo-Indians (which is how she defined herself). When the O'Callaghan's left India in 1948, after Independence, it was the first time they had left the country of their birth, yet they were travelling to somewhere they called 'Home'. Anna said that it was her parent's 'obsession' (her word) with being accepted as English that led to their denial of her background. Funnily enough I had come across a cutting in the *Los Angeles Times* during my research the week before where William had said that Anna's 'dark' looks came from his mother who was born in France. Arguably, the parents fictionalised more of their lives than Anna did. What is so interesting is what compelled them to do that. In the end they paid the heaviest price; they lost their daughter and never met their grandchild.

When we said goodbye Anna was wearing the same outfit she had worn on the three times I saw her; a 'Dennis the Menace' jumper and thin silken trousers. I think, I felt, she was glad that I had taken the trouble to visit her, to listen to her side of the story. I can't remember now what we said beyond that I would come back and that we'd keep in touch. Meeting Anna was important because she became real. I had thought that if I got the chance to interview her I would get an orderly set of answers to an orderly set of questions. But that isn't what happened and was not, I realised, the point. She didn't contact me when I had originally written to her because that was beyond her – she was suing her dead son's ex-girlfriend who was, in turn, counter-suing her – or it might have been the other way around. She was fighting with a woman who continually parked outside her home, and with a man who had charged her $100 to clear some rubbish from the garden and who was in cahoots with the man who ran the car park at the entrance to the trailer park. In short, she had a lot going on and most of it, aside from her painting and sewing, felt chaotic and difficult. She was a woman filled with grief but had nowhere to put that grief. Was this because when she was twenty-three the sky fell in on her world and, by the time she emerged from under the debris, she was an addict and an alcoholic and without a shred of power? Power to change her circumstances, to rebuild her life or to challenge any of the missiles thrown at her. Robert Evans, the film producer, called her 'Marlon's crazed ex-wife' and perhaps she was.[1] And she did some unthinkable things – in relation to her son, at least. But ultimately she illuminated a story which is almost entirely forgotten, just as she herself is almost entirely forgotten. It's a political story and a personal tragedy. Meeting Anna, our 'collaboration' of sorts, put a face to it and provided a piece of surreal colour – and a weirdly charming memory. She is what happens when life chews you up and spits you out as far as it can, and you don't die.

I wrote to Anna several times after we met but I don't know whether she ever received the letters. When I sent a birthday present of some paintbrushes they arrived back around ten months later with 'no longer at this address' scrawled on the package. In the end there was no news until the final news. On the morning of 16th August 2015, I woke up to an email which said that she had died in the town of Kalama in Washington State – a long, long way from Cardiff and Calcutta – taking the facts and fictions of her life with her.

Note

This chapter draws upon the author's unpublished interviews with Anna Kashfi and her experience of meeting her in April 2009.

Notes

[1] Robert Evans, *The Kid Stays in The Picture*, (Faber and Faber, 2004), p. 5

Family Trees

SHRIEVES FAMILY

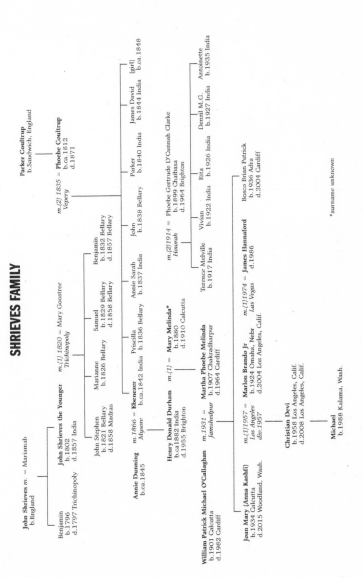

John Shrieves *m.* = Mariamab
b.England
d.1797 Trichinopoly

Parker Coultrup
b.Sandwich, England

Benjamin
b.1796
d.1797 Trichinopoly

John Shrieves the Younger
b.1802
d.1857 India

m.(1) 1820 = Mary Goostree
Trichinopoly

m.(2) 1835 = Phoebe Coultrup
Vepery   b.ca.1812
                        d.1871

John Stephen
b.1821 Bellary
d.1858 Madras

Marianne
b.1826 Bellary

Samuel
b.1829 Bellary
d.1858 Bellary

Benjamin
b.1832 Bellary
d.1857 Bellary

Parker
b.1840 India

James David
b.1844 India

[girl]
b.ca. 1848

Annie Dunning
b.ca.1845

Priscilla
b.ca.1842 India

Annie Sarah
b.1837 India

John
b.1838 Bellary

m.1866 = Ebenezer
Mysore

m.(1) = Mary Melinda*
          b.1880
          d.1910 Calcutta

m.(2)1914 = Phoebe Gertrude D'Ounnah Clarke
Howrah   b.1899 Chaibasa
               d.1964 Brighton

Henry Donald Durham
b.ca1882 India
d.1955 Brighton

m.(1) = Martha Phoebe Melinda
          b.1907 Chakradharpur
          d.1964 Cardiff

Terence Melville
b.1917 India

Vivian
b.1922 India

Rita
b.1926 India

Denzil M.G.
b.1927 India

Antoinette
b.1935 India

William Patrick Michael O'Callaghan
b.1901 Calcutta
d.1982 Cardiff

m.1931 =
Jamshedpur

Bosco Brian Patrick
b.1936 Adra
d.2004 Cardiff

Joan Mary (Anna Kashfi)
b.1934 Calcutta
d.2015 Woodland, Wash.

m.(1)1957 = Marlon Brando Jr
Los Angeles   b.1924 Omaha, Nebr
div.1957   d.2004 Los Angeles, Calif.

m.(1)1974 = James Hannaford
Las Vegas   d.1986

Christian Devi
b.1958 Los Angeles, Calif.
d.2008 Los Angeles, Calif.

Michael
b.1988 Kalama, Wash.

*surname unknown

251

O'CALLAGHAN FAMILY

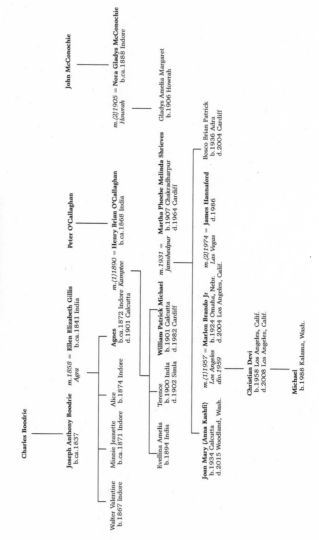

A Guide to the Place Names Connected to the Shrieves and O'Callaghan Families

ADRA is a town in the Purulia district of West Bengal in Eastern India. It was originally best known for 90% of its population being Anglo-Indian and is an important railway junction. Bosco O'Callaghan was born there when his father was promoted to 'Head Train Controller'.

AGRA is a city on the banks of the Yamuna river in the northern state of Uttar Pradesh. The Taj Mahal, commissioned by the Mughal emperor Shah Jahan, was completed there in 1653. The city became the seat of the British government in India in 1835. In 1858 William O'Callaghan's grandparents, Joseph Boodrie and Ellen Gillis, married in Agra.

BELLARY is a historic city in the Ballari district in Karnataka state around two hundred and twenty-five miles from Bangalore, the state capital. The first protestant missionary, the Rev. John Hands of the London Missionary Society, arrived there in 1810. John Shrieves the Younger was stationed in the city before leaving the army to become an assistant missionary.

BOMBAY (Mumbai) was the official name of the most populous city in India until 1995. It lies on the West coast of India and was originally formed of seven islands which were joined at the instigation of the then Governor of Bombay, William Hornby, in 1782. The project was completed in 1845 and the opening of the Suez Canal in 1869 transformed Bombay into one of the largest seaports in the Arabian Sea.

CALCUTTA (Kolkata) is the capital of the Indian state of West Bengal and is located on the east bank of the Hooghly River. Both William O'Callaghan and his daughter, Joan, were born there.

CHAIBASA is a city in the state of Jharkhand in eastern India. It is 25 km from Chakradharpur and 60 km from Jamshedpur. It where both Phoebe O'Callaghan (Kashfi's mother) and Phoebe Shrieves (Kashfi's step-grandmother) were born.

CHAKRADHARPUR is a small city close to the boundaries of two neighbouring states, Odisha and West Bengal. Its railway station is one of the most important in India – its division being the highest earning in the entire Indian Railways. It houses The Railway Colony township estab-lished during the British era, which covers the major part of Chakradharpur. It is where William and Phoebe O'Callaghan were living when their daughter Joan was born.

DARJEELING was developed by the British in the mid-19th century. It lies in the state of West Bengal. The commercial cultivation of tea began in 1856 and the opening of the Darjeeling Himalayan Railway in 1881 further hastened its expansion. Both Joan and Bosco

O'Callaghan attended boarding schools in the area for nine months of each year.

HOWRAH (Haora) is an industrial city on the west bank of the Hoogli River and is connected by bridge to Calcutta. Howrah Junction railway station, one of six in the city, is the oldest station and largest railway complex in India (it has twenty three platforms). It's where William O'Callaghan's father, Henry, married his second wife (William's step-mother) Nora McConochie.

INDORE was founded in 1715 as a trade market on the Narmada River and is now the fourteenth largest city in India. The railway was built in 1875 and the first master-plan of the city was made by the Scottish architect Patrick Geddes in 1918. Both William's mother, Agnes, and his step-mother, Nora, were born in Indore.

JAMSHEDPUR. In 1919 the Viceroy of India, Lord Chelmsford, renamed the city after the pioneering Indian industrialist, Jamsetji Tata, founder of Tata Steel, who died in 1904. India's first steel plant was built in what was the village of Sakchi at the confluence of the Kharkai and Subarnarekha rivers. In 1931 William O'Callaghan married Phoebe Shrieves in the city.

KAMPTEE (Kampthi) was founded in 1821 as a military cantonment by the British on the banks of the Kanhan River. It became an important centre for trade but with the arrival of the railway in the late 19th century the trade was diverted to the nearby city of Nagpur. Today

Kamptee is an outer suburb of Nagpur. Henry O'Callaghan (William's father) married Agnes Boodrie (William's mother) in Kamptee in 1890.

MADRAS (Chennai), located on the Coromandel Coast off the Bay of Bengal, is the capital of the Indian state of Tamil Nadu. Under British rule the city grew into a major naval base and became the central administrative centre for the British in South India. Phoebe O'Callaghan's great grandfather's oldest son John Stephen Shrieves died in Madras in 1858.

MYSORE (Mysuru) is a city at the base of the Chamundi Hills about 146 km southwest of the state capital Bangalore. It's noted for its palaces and its major industry is tourism. Ebenezer Shrieves, Phoebe O'Callaghan's grand-father, married Annie Dunning in Mysore in 1866. In 1897 an outbreak of bubonic plague killed nearly half the population of the city.

SIMLA (Shimla) is the largest city in the northern Indian state of Himachal Pradesh. In 1864, Simla became the summer capital of the British Raj succeeding Murree, northeast of Rawalpindi. It hosted the Simla Accord of 1914 (a treaty concerning the status of Tibet) and the Simla Conference of 1945, a meeting between the Viceroy and the major political leaders of British India. After Independence Simla became the capital of Punjab. In 1902 William O'Callaghan's older brother Terence died, aged two, in Simla.

TRICHINOPOLY (Tiruchirappalli) is a city in the state of Tamil Nadu. It was an important British stronghold during the Carnatic Wars and conquered by the British East India Company in 1801. It was also an important silk-weaving centre. John Shrieves the Younger married Mary Goostree in Trichinopoly in 1820 before moving to Bellary.

VEPERY is a neighbourhood which was developed during the British settlement in the city of Madras (Chennai). Christian missionaries began arriving in the neighbourhood in 1749. The Vepery Mission is the oldest mission connected with the Church of England in India. John Shrieves the Younger married his second wife, Phoebe Coultrup the daughter of missionary Parker Coultrup, in Vepery in 1835

Bibliography

Primary Sources

Broughton, Sarah (2009) *Unpublished Recorded Interviews with Anna Kashfi: (1) 4th April 2009, (2) 6th April 2009, (3) 8th April 2009*, Alpine, California.

Broughton, Sarah (2008) *Unpublished Recorded Interview with Sister Thomasina O'Driscoll*, Newport, South Wales.

Broughton, Sarah (2016) *Unpublished Recorded Interview with Jennifer Mollan Broughton,* Cardiff, South Wales.

Broughton, Sarah (2016) *Unpublished Recorded Interview with Maureen Barry*, Cardiff, South Wales.

Asia, Pacific and Africa Collections at the British Library.

The Academy of Motion Picture Arts and Sciences Margaret Herrick Library, Anna Kashfi Archive, Hedda Hopper Archive.

London Missionary Society.

Glamorgan Records Office.

Secondary Sources

Abram, David et al (2005) *The Rough Guide to India*, London, Rough Guides.

Allen, Jane (2002) *Pier Angeli: a Fragile Life*, Jefferson, McFarland & Company.

Almeida, Rochelle (2017) *Britain's Anglo-Indians: The Invisibility of Assimilation*, Lanham, Lexington Books.

Anthony, Frank (2007) *Britain's Betrayal in India: The Story of the Anglo-Indian Community,* London, Simon Wallenberg Press.

Ardizzone, Heidi (2008) 'Catching Up with History: Night of the Quarter Moon, the Rhinelander Case, and Interracial Marriage in 1959', in Mary Beltran and Camilla Fojas (eds) *Mixed Race Hollywood*, New York, New York University Press.

Barzman, Norma (2005) *The Red and the Blacklist*, Kimarnock, Friction Books.

Basinger, Jeanine (2009) *The Star Machine*, New York, Vintage Books.

Biskind, Peter (2000) *Seeing Is Believing: How Hollywood Taught Us To Stop Worrying And Love The Fifties*, London, Bloomsbury.

Blunt, Alison (2005) *Domicile and Diaspora: Anglo-Indian Women and the Spatial Politics of Home*, Oxford, Blackwell Publishing.

Bly, Nellie (1994) *Marlon Brando: Larger Than Life*, New York, Pinnacle Books.

Borkowski, Mark (2008) *The Fame Formula: How Hollywood's Fixer's, Fakers and Star Makers Created the Celebrity Industry*, London, Pan Macmillan.

Bosworth, Patricia (2009) *Marlon Brando*, London, Weidenfeld & Nicolson.

Brando, Marlon (1994) *Brando: Songs My Mother Taught Me*, with Robert Lindsey, London, Century.

Buettner, Elizabeth (2004) *Empire Families: Britons and Late Imperial India*, Oxford, Oxford University Press.

Buntin, John (2014) *L.A. Noir*, London, Orion Books.

Burton, Richard (2012) *The Richard Burton Diaries*, ed. Chris Williams, London, Yale University Press.

Caplan, Lionel (2001) *Children of Colonialism: Anglo-Indians in a Postcolonial World*, Oxford, Berg.

Carey, Gary (1985) *Marlon Brando: The Only Contender*, London: Robson Books.

BIBLIOGRAPHY

Churchwell, Sarah (2004) *The Many Lives of Marilyn Monroe*, London, Granta.

Christie's (2005) *The Personal Property of Marlon Brando: Thursday 30th June 2005*, New York, Christie's.

Coen, Franklin (1959) *Night of the Quarter Moon*, London, Corgi Books.

Crivello, Kirk (1990) *Fallen Angels: The Lives and Untimely Deaths of 14 Hollywood Beauties*, London, Futura Publications.

Davidson, Bill (1988) *Spencer Tracy: Tragic Idol*, New York, E. P. Dutton.

Davis, Mike (2006) *City of Quartz*, London, Verso.

Davis, Ronald L. (1993) *The Glamour Factory*, Dallas, Southern Methodist University Press, 1993.

deCordova, Richard (2001) *Picture Personalities: The Emergence of the Star System in America*, Champaign, University of Illinois Press.

Dmytryk, Edward (1978) *It's A Hell Of A Life But Not A Bad Living: A Hollywood Memoir*, New York, TIMES BOOKS.

Dors, Diana (1983) *Dors By Diana: An Intimate Self-Portrait*, London, Futura.

Downing, David (1984) *Marlon Brando*, New York, Stein And Day.

Englund, George (2010) *The Naked Brando*. London, Gibson Square.

Evans, Robert (2004) *The Kid Stays In The Picture*, London, Faber and Faber Limited.

Fane-Saunders, Kilmeny (ed.) (2000) *Radio Times Guide to Films*, London, BBC Worldwide Limited.

Finch, Christopher and Rosenkrantz, Linda (1979) *Gone Hollywood: The Movie Colony in the Golden Age*, London, Weidenfeld & Nicolson.

Finler, Joel W. (2003) *The Hollywood Story*, London, Wallflower Press.

Fleming, E.J. (2005) *The Fixers: Eddie Mannix, Howard Strickling and the MGM Publicity Machine*, Jefferson, McFarland & Company, Inc.

Freedland, Michael with Paskin, Barbra (2009) *Witch-Hunt In Hollywood*, London, JR Books.

Friedrich, Otto (1986) *City of Nets: A Portrait of Hollywood in the 1940's*, New York, Harper & Row.

Gates, Phyllis and Bob Thomas (1987) *My Husband, Rock Hudson*, New York, Doubleday & Company.

Gin, Ooi Keat (ed.) (1997) *Japanese Empire in the Tropics Volume 1: Selected Documents and Reports of the Japanese Period in Sarawak, Northwest Borneo, 1941-1945*, Athens OH, Ohio University Monographs in International Studies.

Gledhill, Christine (ed.) (1991) *Stardom: Industry of Desire*, London, Routledge.

Heinmann, Jim and Starr, Kevin (2009) *Los Angeles: Portrait of A City*, Cologne, Taschen.

Hennessy, Peter (2006) *Never Again: Britain 1945-51*, London, Penguin Books.

Higham, Charles (1987) *Brando: The Unauthorized Biography*, New York, New American Library.

Hogan, Peter (2008) *Shirley Bassey: Diamond Diva*, London, André Deutsch.

Iverson, Leslie (2006) *Speed, Ecstasy, Ritalin: The Science of Amphetamines*, Oxford, Oxford University Press.

Iverson, Les (2016) *Drugs: A Very Short Introduction*, Oxford, Oxford University Press.

Jacobs, Chip and Kelly, William J. (2008) *Smogtown: The Lung-Burning History of Pollution in Los Angeles*, Woodstock, The Overlook Press.

BIBLIOGRAPHY

James, Lawrence (1997) *Raj: The Making Of British India*, London, Abacus.

Jessel, David and James Morton, Bill Waddell, Colin Wilson (1991) *Murder Casebook: Starbabies. Cheryl Crane and Christian Brando: Two wild Hollywood children who briefly stole the limelight*. London: Marshall Cavendish Partworks Ltd.

Jordan, Glenn (2001) *'Down The Bay': Picture Post, Humanist Photography and Images of 1950s Cardiff*. Cardiff, Butetown History & Arts Centre.

Jordan, René (1975) *Marlon Brando*, London, W.H. Allen.

Kanfer, Stefan (2008) *Somebody: The Reckless Life and Remarkable Career of Marlon Brando*, New York: Faber and Faber.

Kashfi Brando, Anna and Stein, E. P. (1979) *Brando for Breakfast*, New York, Crown Publishers, Inc.

Kashfi Brando, Anna and Stein, E. P. (1980) *Brando for Breakfast*, New York, Berkley.

Kashner, Sam and MacNair, Jennifer (2003) *The Bad and the Beautiful: Hollywood in the Fifties*, New York: Norton.

Koper, Richard (2015) *Fifties Blondes: Sexbombs, Sirens, Bad Girls and Teen Queens*, Albany, BearManor Media. Kindle Edition.

Kynaston, David (2007) *Austerity Britain*, London, Bloomsbury.

Kynaston, David (2015) *Modernity Britain 1957-62*, London, Bloomsbury.

Laing, Olivia (2014) *The Trip To Echo Spring: On Writers and Drinking*, Edinburgh, Cannongate.

Leamer, Laurence (1986) *As Time Goes By: The Life Of Ingrid Bergman*, London, Hamish Hamilton.

Lenburg, Jeff (1983) *Peekaboo: The Story of Veronica Lake*, New York, St. Martin's Press.

Macnab, Geoffrey (2000) *Searching For Stars*, London, Cassell.

McDonald, Paul (2000) *The Star System*, London, Wallflower.

Mann, William J. (2014) *Tinseltown: Murder, Morphine, And Madness At The Dawn of Hollywood*, New York, HarperCollins.

Mansfield, Michael (2009) *Memoirs of a Radical Lawyer*, London, Bloomsbury Publishing Plc.

Manso, Peter (1994) *Brando*, London, Weidenfeld & Nicolson.

Mason, Philip (1997) *The Men Who Ruled India*, Calcutta, Rupa & Co.

Masters, John (1983) *Bhowani Junction*, London, Sphere Books.

Marchak, Alice (2008) *Me and Marlon: A Memoir*, Ashland, BookMasters, Inc.

Morgan, Dennis (2001) *The Cardiff Story*, Tonypandy, Hackman Print.

Parish, James Robert (2011) *The Hollywood Book of Extravagance: The Totally Infamous, Mostly Disastrous, and Always Compelling Excesses of America's Film and TV Idols*, New Jersey, John Wiley & Sons.

Porter, Darwin (2005) *Brando Unzipped: Bad Boy, Megastar, Sexual Outlaw*, Blood Moon Productions, Ltd.

Reid, Walter (2016) *Keeping The Jewel In The Crown: The British Betrayal of India*, Edinburgh, Birlinn.

Remnick, David (ed.) (2000) *Life Stories: Profiles From The New Yorker*, New York, Random House.

Richard, Cliff (2008) *My Life, My Way*, London, Headline Review.

Richard, Cliff and Shaw, Kate (1998) *Cliff Richard: A Celebration*, Oxford, Isis Publishing.

BIBLIOGRAPHY

Ross, Stephen J. (2011) *Hollywood Left and Right: How Movie Stars Shaped American Politics*, Oxford, Oxford University Press.

Sarris, Andrew (ed.) (1971) *Hollywood Voices*, London, Martin Secker & Warburg.

Seaman, Barbara (1996) *Lovely Me: The Life of Jacqueline Susann*, New York, Seven Stories Press.

Schatz, Thomas (1996) *The Genius Of The System: Hollywood Filmmaking In The Studio Era*, Minneapolis, University of Minnesota Press.

Shaw, Sam (1979) *Brando: In The Camera Eye*, New York, Exeter.

Shipman, David (1989) *Marlon Brando*, London, Sphere Books.

Spencer, Ian R. G. (1997) *British Immigration Policy Since 1939: The Making of Multi-Racial Britain*, London, Routledge.

Susann, Jacqueline (2003) *Valley of the Dolls*, London, Virago; first published by Bernard Gei in 1966.

Stein. Jean (2016) *West Of Eden: An American Place*, London, Jonathan Cape.

Sweet, Matthew (2005) *Shepperton Babylon: The Lost Worlds of British Cinema*, London, Faber and Faber.

Tanitch, Robert (2004) *Brando*, London, Cassell Illustrated.

Thomas, Tony (1991) *The Films of Kirk Douglas*, New York, Citadel Press.

Thompson, David (2003) *Marlon Brando*. New York: DK Publishing.

Thorpe, Edward (1983) *Chandlertown: The Los Angeles of Philip Marlowe*, New York, St. Martin's Press.

Tone, Andrea (2009) *The Age of Anxiety: A History of America's Turbulent Affair with Tranquilizers*, New York, Basic Books.

Tosches, Nick (1992) *Dino: Living High in the Dirty Business of Dreams*. London, Martin Secker & Warburg.

Turner, Steve (1998) *Cliff Richard: The Biography*, Oxford, Lion Publishing.

Wagner, Robert and Scott Eyman (2009) *Pieces of My Heart*, London, Hutchinson.

Walker, Alexander (1974) *Stardom: The Hollywood Phenomenon*, London, Penguin Books.

Walls, Jeanette (2000) *Dish: The Inside Story On The World Of Gossip*, New York, Avon Books.

Wharton, Gary (1997) *Ribbon of dreams: Remembering the Cardiff Cinemas*, Wakefield, Mercia Cinema Society.

Williams, John L. (2010) *Miss Shirley Bassey*, London, Quercus.

Wood, Gaby (2004) 'In Lana Turner's Bedroom', in Ian Jack (ed.), *Film*, London, Granta.

Acknowledgements

Thanks, first and foremost, to the now sadly deceased Anna Kashfi for living so rich and contentious a life – and for her generosity with her time and memories when I interviewed her.

Many thanks to Literature Wales for the Writers' Bursary which enabled me to travel to America to meet Anna Kashfi and to do valuable research at the Margaret Herrick Library in the Fairbanks Center for Motion Picture Study in Los Angeles. Thanks also to the Tyrone Guthrie Centre in Ireland for allowing me space and a beautiful environment in which to gather my thoughts.

To Catherine Merriman and Rob Middlehurst for their unswerving faith in *Brando's Bride* and their support, enthusiasm and wise counsel over many years.

I would also like to thank Tony Curtis, Philip Gross, Chris Meredith, Gillian Clarke and Des Barry for their interest in this book during our time together at the University of South Wales. And to my cohort: Karen Lee Street, Soraya Marr and Holly Müller for the friendship, advice, late nights and occasional dancing. And a special appreciation to Shauna Busto Gilligan for her reading and re-reading of the drafts, attention to detail, incisive comments, shared stories and happy times.

For assorted conversations about Anglo-Indians, invisibility and memories of India I'd like to thank Maureen Barry, David and Anna Hailes, Steve McClarence, Clare Jenkins and Sister Thomasina O'Driscoll. And to Brenda

Caldwell Stewart and Barney's mum, Doreen, for sharing memories of post-war Cardiff.

Particular thanks are due to Rosemary Boyns for finding her way through the maze that is the Shrieves and O'Callaghan family trees. And to Dorothy O'Connor, for her lifelong friendship and for sharing her wealth of knowledge about Los Angeles, and to Patrick O'Connor for dinner at the Brown Derby.

My heartfelt thanks: for reading various drafts along the rocky road to Iris and Rolf Kruger, Valerie Croft, Edith Southwell and Michael Blayney; to Jade Adams for being the finest copy editor and reader anyone could have, and to Matthew Adams, Jessica & Jon Broughton-Humphries, Lloyd and Cai Broughton, Nick & Desirée Broughton, Mavis and Graham Rigby and Betty & Les Phillips.

And to friends that have encouraged me throughout this journey: Laura Watson Cox, Viv Goldberg, Sue Perry-Grech, Sian Roderick, Inge Hanson, Christina Macaulay, Tessa Hughes, Jo Wynne Williams, Cadi & Begw Jones, Lauren Sagar, Warren & Tony Lakin, Kerrie Thomas, Debra Reay, Eddie Ladd, Robbie & Elen Bowman, Jenny Hammerton, Francesca Rhydderch, Clare Lodder, Louise Knowles and Susan & James Wood. And to Wayne & Tess Garvie for the Italian dream.

A special thankyou to Daniel Jones: for everything along this particular way including being the best companion on the American trip, and for the homemade cherry cakes.

Many thanks to all the team at Parthian: particularly to Richard Davies.

My deepest appreciation goes to my parents: Jennifer Mollan Broughton for painstakingly researching our family history during the hardest time in her life, and for her unending love and support, and to Patrick Broughton who kept me going, even after he was gone.

And, finally, to Suzanne Phillips for her beautiful heart and brilliant brain – and for making everything possible.

Illustrations